"Paul Von Blum has given a tremendous gift in bringing the historic sojourn of Paul Robeson to a wide public readership. Robeson's legacy of brilliance, political courage and artistry—captured in word and image here—beckons all of us to draw inspiration from one of the great radical heroes of the 20th century."

> —Scot Brown, History Department, UCLA, author of *Fighting for US: Maulana Karenga, the US Organization, and Black Cultural Nationalism*

"Paul Von Blum has given us a lively and highly accessible biography of one of the most important African American political and cultural figures of the 20th century. This is must reading for anyone interested in the life and times of that remarkable man, Paul Robeson."

> —Steven J. Ross, History Department, University of Southern California, author of *Hollywood Left and Right: How Movie Stars Shaped American Politics*

"The world should know the truth about Paul Robeson, one of the greatest Americans of all time. *Paul Robeson For Beginners* helps to restore him to his honored place as a giant artist and activist of the 20th century."

> —Leon Bibb, folksinger, actor, and longtime friend of Paul Robeson

PAUL ROBESON
FOR BEGINNERS

PAUL ROBESON
FOR BEGINNERS

BY **PAUL VON BLUM**

ILLUSTRATIONS BY
ELIZABETH VON NOTIAS
& RAMSESS

FOR BEGINNERS®

For Beginners LLC
155 Main Street, Suite 211
Danbury, CT 06810 USA
www.forbeginnersbooks.com

A For Beginners® Documentary Comic Book
Copyright © 2013

Cataloging-in-Publication information is available from the Library of Congress.

ISBN # 978-1-934389-81-2 Trade

Manufactured in the United States of America

For Beginners® and Beginners Documentary Comic Books® are published by For Beginners LLC.

First Edition

10 9 8 7 6 5 4 3 2 1

contents

Chapter 1:
INTRODUCTION

PAUL ROBESON WAS ONE OF THE GREATEST RENAISSANCE persons in American history. An exceptional scholar, lawyer, athlete, stage and screen actor, linguist, singer, and civil rights and political activist, he performed brilliantly in every professional enterprise he undertook. Few human beings have achieved his levels of excellence in one field, much less several. Any serious consideration of civil rights and radical politics as well as American sports, musical, theatrical and film history must consider the enormous contributions of Paul Robeson.

And yet, Paul Robeson remains virtually unknown by millions of educated Americans. People typically know him for only one, if any, of the major successes of his life: the concert singer best known for "Ol' Man River," the star of Shakespeare's *Othello* on Broadway in the early 1940s, or the political activist blacklisted for his radical views and activism during the era of McCarthyism in the 1950s.

From the late 1950s until the centennial of his birth in 1998, Paul Robeson remained frozen out of the national consciousness, even though he was the most well recognized African American in the world during the 1930s and 1940s. His multifaceted talents were overlooked by his increasingly unpopular political activities; his support for the Soviet Union made him a pariah in his native land during the Cold War following the defeat of the Axis powers. He was excised from the history books, an erasure reminiscent of Stalinist-era removal of "enemies" from photographs and other official Soviet documents. His disappearance from the official record, including from school textbooks and references in mainstream media sources, constituted an egregious example of reputational censorship in the twentieth century. This tragic reality has prevented millions of Americans from understanding Robeson's contributions to American cultural and political life. As historian Joseph Dorinson ruefully noted, "Paul Robeson is the greatest legend nobody knows."

The irony of Robeson's disappearance from public consciousness is striking and tragic. Members of the general public and prominent personalities alike held Paul Robeson in the highest regard, including world-renowned political and cultural figures like Eleanor Roosevelt, W.E.B. Du Bois, Pablo Neruda, Sergei Eisenstein, Jomo Kenyatta, Jawaharlal Nehru and many more. American athletic and entertainment figures like Joe Louis, Canada Lee, Lena Horne, Dizzy Gillespie, Zero Mostel, Odetta, Sidney Poitier, Harry Belafonte, James Earl Jones and scores of others viewed Robeson as a cultural giant and moral role model, whose trailblazing efforts paved the way for decades of African American advancement in every walk of life. When Paul Robeson's life ended in loneliness and obscurity in 1976, a deep stain on American history surfaced dramatically with the media announcements of his death. This stain will take decades to wash out of the American social fabric.

The long overdue restoration process has begun. Several events and creative developments converged after Robeson's death to propel him back into national recognition, and reverse the process of reputational obliteration. An early example occurred in 1978 when Phillip Hays Dean wrote and produced the play "Paul Robeson." This dramatic effort chronicled the life of Paul Robeson from his childhood to his death, and focused on the racism he encountered and combated in every aspect of his life and career. Numerous actors played the starring role of Robeson, notably James Earl Jones, Ben Guillory and Avery Brooks. While the play was not without its share of controversies and mixed critical responses, it exposed Robeson's life and work to audiences, many of which were uneducated about his accomplishments.

The 1979 production and release of the short documentary "Tribute to an Artist," which Saul J. Turrell directed and Sidney Poitier narrated, continued the process of public reeducation about Paul Robeson. This engaging film, which received the Academy Award for Documentary Short Subject in 1980, chronicled Robeson's versatile life as an athlete, artist and activist, as well as his blacklisting, relying on news and film clips, interview segments and photographic still shots. The presence of the universally respected and admired Poitier in this documentary added substantial gravitas to the project and bolstered the drive to restore Robeson's presence in American cultural and political history.

"Official" Hollywood also acknowledged Paul Robeson in 1979. The Hollywood Walk of Fame consists of more than 2,400 five-pointed stars embedded in the sidewalks of Hollywood Boulevard and Vine Street in Hollywood, California. These stars represent achievement in every aspect of the entertainment industry. Honorees include actors, directors, producers, musicians and more. The Hollywood Chamber of Commerce administers the Walk of Fame and the Hollywood Historic trust maintains it. In 1978, the selection committee, reflecting the anti-Robeson bias of the era, voted against a star for him. Widespread protest from more enlightened entertainers, politicians and civic leaders caused the committee to reverse its decision and a Robeson star was installed.

In 1980, the Recording Academy inducted Robeson into the Grammy Hall of Fame for "Ballad for Americans." Eighteen years later, in 1998, Robeson received an actual Grammy posthumously, thereby solidifying his belated recognition as a premier vocal artist of his time. These honors that acknowledged and celebrated Paul Robeson's exemplary musical talents propelled him back into the public arena after decades of forced obscurity.

Higher education entered the Robeson revival arena in 1988 when the UCLA African American Studies Center offered the first university course focusing entirely on Paul Robeson. Entitled "Paul Robeson: An American Life," this interdisciplinary course opened with "Tribute to an Artist" and covered the essential aspects of Robeson's life and career. The course attracted undergraduate and graduate students of all racial and ethnic backgrounds, and because it was well received, the course was offered every year for more than fifteen years. More importantly, the UCLA Robeson course was initiated at the dawn of the Internet era. By the early 1990s, its syllabus became available on several websites and other institutions began making it accessible to faculty and students worldwide. The course instructor made numerous presentations about the class in scholarly conventions and popular venues, and published articles in professional journals about its existence and success.

Likewise, in 1988, Beacon Press reissued Robeson's 1958 account of his life and political views, *Here I Stand*. On its original publication in 1958, *Here I Stand* was largely ignored in the mainstream press and reviewed almost exclusively in African American newspapers and magazines and in left-wing publications. With an introduction by historian Sterling Stuckey, one of the few Robeson scholars in the United States at the time, the new edition was well received and widely reviewed.

The 1989 publication of Martin Bauml Duberman's magisterial biography, *Paul Robeson*, marked a powerful turning point in reversing the Cold War obliteration of Paul Robeson from the historical record. A distinguished and prolific historian, Duberman drew on a vast array of primary sources, including family papers, letters to and from Robeson, interviews, government documents and other records to provide a sweeping view of Robeson's life. The biography presented a highly favorable view of Robeson while also addressing some of the more problematic features of his personal life, including his long record of marital infidelity, and his psychiatric struggles. While this narrative disturbed some of his more zealous admirers, it humanized Robeson's accomplishments by putting them into the context of a man who struggled to transcend the adversity of his personal life.

Duberman's biography was favorably reviewed throughout the scholarly press and the mass media. It helped catalyze Robeson's reentry into intellectual life. He was once again a respectable subject of discourse in serious academic circles.

The athletic world also took steps to remedy the long historical injustice when Robeson was enshrined in the College Football Hall of Fame in 1995, seventy-seven years after his greatest triumphs on the gridiron at Rutgers University. It is not unusual for Hall of Fame inductees to wait, sometimes for several years, for formal recognition of past athletic achievements. In Robeson's case, however, this protracted delay had nothing to do with ambiguity or controversy over his collegiate football brilliance. It had everything, on the contrary, to do with his political unpopularity and blacklisting in the post-war era. Nevertheless, the 1995 action constituted another step in the reputational rehabilitation.

The most significant factor in restoring Paul Robeson's reputation occurred in 1998, and it resulted from the massive national and international celebrations for the centennial of his birth. There were approximately 400 joyous affairs, usually complete with visual and musical expressions celebrating Robeson's career in numerous fields. Frequently, Robeson's friends and associates, including fellow victims of Cold War blacklisting, made dramatic appearances. Celebration committees were established in several American cities and throughout the world, while film showings, plays, concerts and other performances marked the one hundredth anniversary of his birth on April 9, 1998. Some of these centennial committees remain in operation and have sponsored community programs that reinforce contemporary memories of Paul Robeson, and bring his legacy to students and young people who may receive, even now, inadequate exposure to accomplished persons of color in their education.

In New York, in February 1998, Long Island University sponsored a well-attended Paul Robeson Conference that attracted scholars, students, labor leaders and multigenerational members of the general public. Several other colleges and universities held panel discussions and related events to reinforce academic interest in Paul Robeson. Many of these activities received substantial media coverage and numerous publications and curricular materials about Robeson and his life appeared shortly thereafter.

Centennial events were also held in Switzerland, the United Kingdom, Finland, Germany, Norway, Russia, Portugal, Israel, Australia and elsewhere during that time. These international celebrations reinforced the American "reincarnation" of Paul Robeson's reputation. His removal from the historical record did not exist throughout much of the rest of the world, a reality that caused many American newspaper and magazine readers and television viewers to wonder how a man of such stunning talent could have faded so dramatically from public view. The international celebrations in 1998 reflected the isolation of the American destruction of Paul Robeson's powerful life and legacy and brought increased attention to the unsavory era of McCarthyism in American national history.

The belated issuance of a Robeson US postage stamp in 2004 constituted an oblique public apology and encouraged others to explore his diverse artistic and political contributions. Other countries had previously issued postage stamps honoring Robeson, including the German Democratic Republic (formerly East Germany),

Guyana, and Mali. The US version was the twenty-seventh stamp in the Black Heritage Series, resulting from a lengthy and frustrating political struggle that lasted eight years. The campaign for a Robeson stamp, launched by legendary folk singer Pete Seeger in 1996, attracted almost one hundred thousand signatures on petitions to the Citizens' Stamp Advisory Committee, the entity that evaluates and recommends subjects for new United States postage stamps. Petitions were regularly circulated at Robeson centennial gatherings, and various other events.

This campaign attracted numerous letters, newspaper editorials and individual letters to the Advisory Committee as well as most members of the Congressional Black Caucus. Eventually, this political pressure succeeded, and the first stamp unveiling occurred at Princeton University on January 20, 2004, with Paul Robeson, Jr. in attendance. Similar unveilings occurred in New York, Chicago, Los Angeles, Oakland, San Francisco and elsewhere, often organized by local Paul Robeson centennial groups. These festive events usually included brief presentations by political figures, community leaders and academics, and were accompanied by musical performances featuring Robeson songs.

In 2005, moreover, Lafayette College in Pennsylvania organized an international conference, "Paul Robeson: His History and Development as an Intellectual." The gathering attracted scholars, artists and community and labor activists who explored the many dimensions of Robeson's life. A key feature of the Lafayette Conference was the contemporary significance and implications of his work in such fields as theater, film and politics.

Finally, in January 2012, the United States Information Resource Center in Jamaica was named after Paul Robeson, recognizing his 1948 visit to the Caribbean nation, and his continuing stellar reputation throughout that region. With the US Ambassador and Robeson's granddaughter Susan in attendance at the ceremony, this event marked yet another step in Robeson's historical rehabilitation.

By the end of the first decade of the twenty-first century, material on Robeson had proliferated throughout the world. Books and articles about him and various aspects of his life now exist in abundance. His vocal recordings are widely available; listeners have easy access to his magnificent voice and younger people may now hear his singing for the first time. Above all, the Internet is replete with material about Paul Robeson, addressing every feature of his life from 1898 to 1976. A simple Google search yields thousands of results, making it easy for researchers and the general public to rediscover the amazing accomplishments and controversies surrounding one of the most accomplished figures of twentieth-century American life.

The Robeson reputational rehabilitation process, however, is far from complete. The resurgence of interest in his life and work is modest, and millions of ostensibly educated Americans have still never heard of Paul Robeson. College and university teachers regularly report that the mere mention of Robeson evokes puzzled responses from their students. Although historical texts now sometimes make brief note of his efforts in sports, theater, film, music and politics, comprehensive discussions and analyses of those contributions remain scarce.

It is important to explore the deeper reasons for Robeson's long absence from public consciousness. The obvious reason for his disappearance from public view emerged from the anti-communism of the late 1940s and 1950s, often known as McCarthyism. This era has been extensively documented, with compelling firsthand accounts and perceptive scholarly and journalistic treatment. The record of federal and state investigations, loyalty boards and oaths, subversive hunts and FBI informers, political prosecutions, State Department restrictions on travel, censorship of mail and blacklists that led to thousands of people losing their jobs, most notably liberals and leftists in the entertainment industry, government service, journalism, the arts and education, remains a major blight on American history. As historian David Caute noted in his detailed analysis of American anti-communist hysteria in *The Great Fear,* "[t]he wealthiest, most secure nation in the world was sweat-drenched in fear."

Yet of the thousands of people demonized as "communists" during this time, Paul Robeson was among the most viciously attacked, with horrific consequences to his physical and mental health, and to the deeper principles of a constitutional democracy. Robeson was not only blacklisted from his American artistic career on the stage and in the concert hall and recording studio; he had his passport lifted from 1950 to 1958 and was unable to make a living abroad, despite his worldwide fame. He was under surveillance by the FBI from 1941 until near the time of his death. Government investigators harassed his friends and associates, ensuring that major segments of his own African American community would turn away from him, fearful for their own livelihoods and reputations. At the height of McCarthyism, sympathetic commentary about Robeson, even possession of a Robeson phonograph record, was widely regarded as evidence of suspicious conduct and political disloyalty.

Typical U.S. anticommunist literature of the 1950s, specifically addressing the entertainment industry. ca. 1950–56

During the late 1940s and throughout the 1950s, moreover, American foreign policy was driven by paranoia and fear of the Soviet Union. Those policies were inextricably related to the rampant domestic suppression of civil liberties. A longtime Soviet supporter like Paul Robeson inevitably bore the brunt of such policies. His frequent travels to the Soviet Union, his continuing popularity there, and his knowledge of the Russian language all tied him to America's post-World War II supreme enemy. This made his persecution and his obliteration from public consciousness all the more understandable—and entirely justifiable in the eyes of the dominant powers at the time.

Robeson's Soviet sympathies and ties, his close association with the US Communist Party, and his unpopular political views and activism generally during the McCarthy era, however, are insufficient to explain entirely why he was singled out with greater ferocity than most other victims of blacklists and other economic reprisals, government harassment, criminal prosecutions and similar modes of political destruction. The major reason underlying Paul Robeson's persecution and subsequent obliteration from the national consciousness reflects the darkest stain on American history: racism. By the late 1940s and early 1950s, it would have been unseemly to use vulgar racial epithets against Robeson publicly, although racial slurs against him in private were probably common. This was likely the case not only in places like the South, where overtly racist language was still commonplace, but throughout the entire nation, where racial slurs toward African Americans, and actual discriminatory practices in housing, employment, education and elsewhere, often went under the public radar.

The fact remains that Paul Robeson was a black political radical in a problematic period of American history. As such, he was a convenient target and attacks could be mounted against him using popular anti-communist rhetoric that thinly concealed the deeper racial disposition of many of Robeson's adversaries. "Dirty red," "go back to Russia," "commie traitor," "un-American," and similar pejorative terms were acceptable substitutes for overt racist scorn.

The racism against Paul Robeson went deeper than linguistic derision. Strong, accomplished black men had regularly been objects of attack throughout American history. Many had been subjected to allegations of sexual longings and improprieties against white women, a reality that was responsible for lynching black men from the Reconstruction period to the mid-twentieth century. Robeson himself had been accused of this "sin" when he played Othello on the New York stage in the early 1940s because he was a dark-skinned African American kissing Uta Hagen playing Desdemona—the classic miscegena-

Paul Robeson, world famous Negro baritone, leading Moore Shipyard (Oakland, CA) workers in singing the Star Spangled Banner, here at their lunch hour recently, after he told them: ' This is a serious job—winning this war against fascists. We have to be together.' Robeson himself was a shipyard worker in World War I.

tion that frightened, even terrified, millions of white Americans at the time. It was easy to merge these irrational impulses with the national hysteria against subversion, making Robeson an inviting target for his conservative antagonists with multiple motivations and inclinations.

Underlying racism also explains decades of resentment for Paul Robeson for his monumental achievements in several fields. One of many long-standing stereotypes upheld by racist sentiment toward African Americans is that they lack intellect and drive, and that their inherent laziness is a natural impediment to success in the arts and in other professions. Robeson's dramatic repudiation of this racist view and his unapologetic advocacy of African American advancement in a racist society doubtless generated white hostility. The fervent "patriotism" of the post-war era did not repudiate these racist attitudes, which fostered hatred and repressed envy against a man who negated conventional notions about black people. Because it was impossible to openly acknowledge this unnerving psychological reality at the time, racist sentiment toward Robeson was disguised in the form of the anti-communist chorus.

White supremacy remains one of the factors explaining Robeson's continuing lack of public recognition in the first decades of the twenty-first century. Although informational sources about his life are widely available, millions of white Americans still struggle to acknowledge the professional and intellectual superiority of any African American. This reality transcends Robeson himself; it applies to thousands of other accomplished black women and men, who must constantly prove themselves again and again in the face of widespread racial suspicion and skepticism.

Regardless of Paul Robeson's removal from the historical record, and his slow restoration to public knowledge, his story is the story of American political and cultural history in the twentieth century; his life was a quintessentially American life. His excellence in athletics, theater, film and song, as well as his vigorous leadership in the struggle for racial dignity, for labor, for ethnic and racial brotherhood, for African independence and for numerous other progressive social causes, reveal his struggles against the tremendous barriers facing people of African descent in the United States. His subsequent and horrific persecution reveals the frequently dramatic gaps in American history between its democratic and constitutional ideals and its actual practices. The complex, turbulent life of Paul Robeson provides a powerful if somewhat disconcerting view of his native land, while his reputational restoration after death provides hope for a more progressive and understanding future. Both of these views are essential if the mistakes of the recent past are to be avoided in future years, with challenges even more overwhelming than those the nation faced from 1898 to 1976, close at hand.

Chapter 2:
THE EARLY DAYS

THE WORLD WOULD CHANGE DRAMATICALLY DURING THE seventy-seven years of Paul Robeson's remarkable life. Born on April 9, 1898 in Princeton, New Jersey to Rev. William Drew Robeson and Maria Louisa Robeson as the youngest of five children, Robeson came into a society that was only a few decades removed from slavery. As Robeson describes in Here I Stand, Princeton "was spiritually located in Dixie," with dramatic class and racial divisions. The white population, including the faculty and students at its famed University (where blacks were not admitted), enjoyed the privileges of wealth and power, while its black population were there as servants, toiling as cooks, domestics, caretakers and unskilled laborers. Schools were rigidly segregated and Paul Robeson's older brother William had to travel to Trenton to attend high school. Princeton was deeply racist in its attitudes and practices, a legacy that inevitably affected Paul Robeson for the remainder of his life.

This didn't prevent the Robeson family from having a relatively elevated status in the community. Rev. Robeson, as a minister, received respect from members of both racial groups. In 1900, however, after twenty years as pastor of the Witherspoon Street Presbyterian Church, Rev. Robeson was forced out of his church. This major professional blow resulted from an internal conflict, a battle that may have also included some animosity from influential members of Princeton's white community, who were generally unsympathetic to African Americans and who may have been uneasy with Rev. Robeson's public views on social injustice.

Paul Robeson was happy for much of his early childhood, playing with his siblings and learning the athletic skills that would later propel him to stardom. In 1904, when Paul was only six, the Robeson family endured a devastating trauma when his mother, already suffering from ill health and impaired sight, was fatally injured in a fire, after a coal from the stove fell on her dress while she was cleaning a house. She lingered in severe pain for several days before succumbing to her injuries. Throughout his life, Robeson recalled little of his mother except for a vivid memory of her funeral and a more generalized sense of her love, education, and intellect.

By 1907, Rev. Robeson had relocated to Westfield, New Jersey, reestablished himself as a minister, changed denominations and built a small African Methodist Episcopal (AME) Zion church serving a predominantly southern rural black congregation. By 1910, he moved again, creating an AME Zion parish in Somerville, New Jersey. By then, Paul's older siblings had moved away from the Robeson house, and Rev. Robeson became the foremost educational and moral influence in the young Paul Robeson's life—an influence that would inform his subsequent conduct, including the radical political activism that caused him such difficulty and turmoil later in his life.

"The glory of my boyhood years was my father," Robeson writes in his Prologue to *Here I Stand*. The character of Rev. William Drew Robeson undoubtedly shaped Paul from early boyhood. As a young man, he escaped slavery from North Carolina through the Underground Railway. He worked his way through historically and predominantly black Lincoln University to become a minister. Above all, he was a man of powerful personal integrity, moral courage and pride in his race, all traits that he instilled in his son, and that pervaded every feature of Paul Robeson's artistic and political life.

Rev. Robeson spoke infrequently about his early slave experiences and his escape from bondage, but those experiences inevitably had a huge impact on how he raised his son.

They reflect a vision of resistance against oppression and persistence against all forms of racism emerging from the impact of slavery in the United States. Rev. Robeson had no hint of servility in his temperament. Even during the difficult days when he lost his pastorate in Princeton and scrambled to earn a living by hauling ashes and driving a coach, he retained a powerful sense of personal dignity. He taught his son to stand up for principle and to refuse to back down simply for convenience or expediency.

Paul Robeson's father was also deeply committed to rigorous educational standards, providing an enduring lesson for his children. Although Robeson did not recall his father's specific political comments about the debate then raging between the militancy of Dr. W.E.B. Du Bois and the more conservative vision of Booker T. Washington, it was always obvious to him that his father was entirely opposed to Washington's view that blacks should limit their education to technical training alone. Instead, he pushed his son to pursue excellence in *every* feature of the curriculum, including the classic languages of Latin and Greek.

He also instructed his son in the art of oratory, reflecting his own eloquence in the pulpit as well as one of the enduring legacies of the black church. He gave his son speeches to memorize and then cri-

W.E.B. Du Bois, *photograph by Addison N. Scurlock*

tiqued Paul's delivery. This early training led the young Robeson to excel as a speaker and debater throughout high school and college. It also informed his subsequent skills as a political orator in his quest for racial justice, and in his various activities in pursuit of all his political objectives. Likewise, Rev. Robeson encouraged his son's remarkable voice in the church choir and in the high school chorus, a prelude to one of the most brilliant singing careers in modern US and world history.

Rev. Robeson demanded academic perfection from his son, revealing dissatisfaction with any grade lower than "100." This was a demanding yet fully loving standard that inspired his son to use all his talents, especially in pursuing intellectual excellence. At Somerville High School, Robeson formed friendships with white students in an environment with only a few African Americans in the student body. Robeson fit in well, excelling in academics, singing in the glee club, and debating. He also took to the stage in an amateurish partial version of *Othello*, an experience that likely established a foundation for his future professional efforts as an actor in London, Broadway and elsewhere. His remarkable record in high-school sports, moreover (the subject for the next chapter in this volume), increased his personal popularity and was an initial step in the athletic distinction that would propel him to national recognition at Rutgers College.

As a black high-school student, Robeson sought to "act right" in order to get along with everyone, especially in an environment with less overt racism than he would later encounter. This strategy, familiar to minorities throughout American history, carries with it a degree of psychological servitude; Paul Robeson would eventually learn to abandon the mask and assume a more authentic identity as a strong black man.

At Somerville High School, Robeson reported that the most obvious racism he encountered came from his principal, Dr. Ackerman. Scarcely concealing his racist hostility for a young black student who displayed superiority in everything he did, Ackerman responded to each of Robeson's successes with scorn. When Robeson joined the school glee club, for example, the music teacher had to overcome the principal's angry objection to having Paul sing as the soloist. Like many other whites in positions of authority, he resented any African American who challenged his seemingly immutable vision of black racial inferiority. The principal's reaction was painful and puzzling, but it only pushed Robeson to strive harder. It gave him a glimpse of the barriers that he would be forced to address in a world where many people in authority share the intractable racism of Dr. Ackerman, and it likely stirred the rebellious inclinations that soon pervaded much of his life and career. Decades later in *Here I Stand*,

Robeson revealed his understanding of the impact of his racist principal at Somerville High School: "Deep in my heart . . . was a conviction which none of the Ackermans of America would ever be able to shake."

Robeson's siblings had, like his father, major influences on him during his formative years. Paul credited his older brother William Drew, Jr. as the most significant influence in his own ability to study. William spent hours coaching Robeson on the fundamentals of football. His brother Ben also helped inspire Robeson's interests in sports, and both he and sister Marian acted as professional role models by entering the ministry and teaching respectively.

The most intriguing influence came from the most ostensibly unsuccessful Robeson sibling, Reeve (called Reed). Reed was a brawler who rejected any tolerance for racial slurs or slights. He carried a bag of small rocks to sling at privileged whites, including Princeton University students, who treated him as a racial inferior. He engaged in numerous street fights, causing Rev. Robeson severe distress, especially when he had to intervene at the police station to get Reed out of trouble. Eventually, Rev. Robeson told Reed to leave, fearing that he would set a bad example for Paul. Reed wound up in Detroit and died young under murky circumstances.

Years later, Paul Robeson remembered his troubled older brother with love:

"Restless, rebellious, scoffing at the white man's law—I've known many Negroes like Reed. I see them every day. Blindly, in their own reckless manner, they seek a way out for themselves; alone, they pound with their fists and fury against walls that only the shoulders of the many can topple. 'Don't ever take low,' was the lesson that Reed taught me. 'Stand up to them and hit back harder than they hit you!'"

Robeson fully accepted his brother's racial militancy, but he also understood the value of delayed personal gratification, as well as the effectiveness of political organizing in response to racism that went far deeper than individual racial slurs and slights. He expressed this perspective through his accomplishments in the arts, and in the more systematic radical political endeavors of his adult life.

In his senior year at Somerville High School, Paul Robeson took a competitive examination for a four-year scholarship to Rutgers College, and won. Although he would have likely been more comfortable at his father's alma mater, all-black Lincoln University, he accepted the scholarship and enrolled as a freshman in 1915. Rutgers, one of the oldest colleges in the United States, was then a private institution with fewer than 500 students—vastly different from the multi-campus state public institution of the early twenty-first century, which enrolls more than 58,000 students (additionally, its flagship New Brunswick campus hosts, since 1972, the Paul Robeson Cultural Center, which provides educational, cultural and social programs and services for minority students, especially African Americans). Before Robeson enrolled in 1915, only two other black students had attended Rutgers and only one other enrolled during his time on campus.

At seventeen, Robeson, academically and athletically accomplished and still largely unexposed to the deep malevolence of American racism, entered the New Brunswick campus of Rutgers College. Most accounts of his undergraduate experiences focus extensively, even exclusively, on his brilliant athletic record, particularly on his stellar football performances.

College experiences are always significant in a person's intellectual and emotional journey. For Robeson, being the sole black student in an all white institution added additional burdens to the inevitable stresses of collegiate life. This reality, regretfully, has changed marginally in almost a century. Today there is more ethnic and racial diversity in higher education. Nevertheless, African American students still regularly report feelings of alienation and isolation on college campuses. While cases of overt racism are scarce, the deeper, more institutionalized manifestations are readily apparent. For Paul Robeson, his consciousness of his race was a daily reality, especially his desire to be "a credit to his race," a dogma that was deeply felt by African Americans of accomplishment, as well as sympathetic members of the

18

white majority. That belief also imposed additional emotional burdens on the young black, physically imposing student.

At Rutgers, Robeson was required to live alone in one of the college residences. Many white students stared at him disdainfully, even in his classes. He was forced to eat in the school cafeteria by himself, with the servers looking on indifferently. Having been excluded from most campus social events, including many athletic functions, because of his race, Robeson generally used the pretext of having other things to do, thus sparing his own personal discomfort, and the white majority's complicity in racism and white privilege. "Acting right," by white standards under such circumstances carried a major emotional price, and eventually Robeson would aggressively discard this coping strategy.

Robeson completed his freshman year with stellar grades. He continued his academic distinction by becoming one of four undergraduate students to be selected for Phi Beta Kappa as a junior. He displayed oratorical prowess by serving on the varsity debate team, and won several awards for speaking excellence. He also sang for the Rutgers Glee Club, but only under the condition that he only sang at home concerts, and could not attend traveling concerts or social functions. He was also elected to the Literary Society, where he was similarly excluded from some of the social functions because he was black. As a senior, he was inducted into the Cap and Skull honor society, which recognized the best men representing Rutgers College's ideals.

These academic honors all reflected the influence of his father (whose death at 73 on May 17, 1918 grieved the young Paul Robeson) and demonstrated his conviction that his intellectual development occupied a higher priority than his athletic glory, especially for the longer term. Robeson understood, at least intuitively, that his intellect would drive his success in whatever realm he ultimately decided to pursue—in the early years of the twentieth century professional careers in football or other sports were not realistic options for the long term. Robeson's academic priorities remain extremely relevant almost a century later in a university environment where intercollegiate sports occupy a huge role, and where "student-athletes" in the money sports of football and basketball frequently pay marginal attention to their academic obligations.

One of Robeson's key academic accomplishments was his Rutgers senior thesis. He chose as his topic "The Fourteenth Amendment, The Sleeping Giant of the American Constitution," a vision that previewed his early interest in law and that shed light on some of the subsequent legal developments that would affect both race relations and the legal process in the United States. Nothing in that thesis revealed any indication of the black militancy that later dominated his political consciousness. Nor did it reflect an awareness of the growing black militancy of the present times. Rather, its civil and legalistic tone continued to express the young Robeson's desire to fit into the dominant white society.

The thesis represented a call to work within the established system, a vision he later vigorously challenged, but it also revealed a sophisticated understanding of the power of the Fourteenth Amendment to bridge the gap between American ideals of racial equality, and its dismal record in actual practice. It was, after all, during the time of "separate but equal," the infamous doctrine that the United States Supreme Court declared in its 1896 ruling in *Plessy v. Ferguson*.

Although unduly optimistic, his undergraduate thesis revealed the same keen understanding of the equal protection clause of the Fourteenth Amendment that such iconic African American lawyers as Charles Hamilton Houston, Thurgood Marshall and Constance Baker Motley used in arguing and winning such landmark Supreme Court education cases as *Sweatt v. Painter* (1950) and *Brown v. Board of Education* (1954) and the miscegenation case of *Loving v. Virginia* (1967).

Few analysts, especially those with more radical critiques of American capitalism, conclude that any of these decisions fundamentally altered the deeper racism of America that has been embedded in the land since before its inception as a nation and perpetuated throughout its history. The vast majority of African Americans remained mired in poverty and could scarcely enjoy the benefits of Supreme Court proclamations that rhetorically favored their dignity and liberation from discrimination. Still, the legal struggles against segregation, which Robeson foresaw long before their dramatic public successes, were an inseparable feature of the broader civil rights and anti-racist struggles that pervaded American life in the second half of the twentieth century.

On June 19, 1919, to conclude his renowned undergraduate years, Robeson delivered the valedictory address before the graduating class, parents, faculty and distinguished guests. Focusing on "The New Idealism," he spoke of uplifting his people and of his own commitment to that noble objective. Generally cautious and conciliatory, the address nevertheless challenged white America to live up to its obligations regarding the African American

"We, too, of this younger race have a part in this new American Idealism. We too have felt the great thrill of what it means to sacrifice for other than the material. We revere our honored ones as belonging to the martyrs who died, not for personal gain, but for adherence to moral principles, principles which through the baptism of their blood reached a fruitage otherwise impossible, giving as they did a broader conception to our national life. Each one of us will endeavor to catch their noble spirit and together in the consciousness of their great sacrifice consecrate ourselves with whatever power we may possess to the furtherance of the great motives for which they gave their lives."

—FROM PAUL ROBESON'S "THE NEW IDEALISM" VALEDICTORY ADDRESS

minority—the "less favored race," as Robeson put it in his oration. The speech was received with overwhelming approval, allowing the audience, perhaps for the first time, to witness a talented young back man and inviting them to question their lingering notions of black inferiority. Although far from the robust defense of black people in his mature years, the speech provided a glimpse into the emerging racial and political consciousness that would in time pervade his identity. The fact that he had centrally highlighted the topic of race itself, especially in the tumultuous year of 1919, when African Americans were under attack by racist white mobs throughout the nation, was a bold act that foreshadowed his future trajectory.

Reverend Robeson likely imagined that his son Paul would follow him into the ministry, especially given his intellectual and oratorical gifts and the fact that he had worked in the church and occasionally delivered sermons for his father. In college, however, Paul decided that a legal career would be better suited to his increasing belief that he should serve his race. During the next four years, he entered law school, but he also played three seasons of professional football to pay his way for his legal education, worked as an assistant coach for the Rutgers and Lincoln University football teams, played semi-pro basketball, got married to Eslanda Cardoza Goode, made his acting debut on Broadway, sang at numerous churches and community centers and entered the developing and vibrant black cultural scene in Harlem known widely as the Harlem Renaissance.

Robeson's accomplishments were remarkable. Law school, even in the early twentieth century, was demanding and stressful, often requiring fulltime study with little time for external activities, including much recreation. Initially, with the help of his Rutgers football coach Foster Sanford and some influential Rutgers alumni, Robeson received a scholarship to New York University Law School. Deciding that he preferred to be nearer to Harlem, he switched mid-year to Columbia Law School, which had a policy of not accepting transfer students. This decision cost Robeson his scholarship, propelling him to the flurry of activities intended, in substantial part, to cover his educational and living expenses.

The record on Robeson's performance as a law student is sparse; he interrupted his legal education with the other activities that would eventually propel him to international acclaim. But his specific interests and quality of his law school performance were not comparable to those of his undergraduate efforts at Rutgers. Martin Duberman reports that he compiled a mediocre record in law school, with Cs comprising two thirds of his grades. Only a few courses and professors truly captured his full attention and imagination. Few legal subjects could match the broader intellectual engagement of his Rutgers senior thesis that addressed the more personal topic of race in America. He was largely bored with the legal curriculum and distracted by his growing interest in acting and his moneymaking efforts in professional football.

Still, his personal ambivalence led him to try a legal career, despite the fact that his true ambitions were elsewhere. He received his law degree from Columbia University in February of 1923, and after a few months of reflecting about his future, he accepted work as a legal clerk in a law office with the assistance, once again, of his former Rutgers football coach Sanford. He joined the firm of Louis W. Stotesbury, a Rutgers alumnus who headed a prominent firm specializing in estates and wills—not exactly a subject that could generate a sustained interest in a person of Paul Robeson's broad interests and artistic inclinations.

But Robeson made a strong attempt to perform his duties in an environment where he was the sole black employee. His initial assignment was to draft a brief of a highly visible case involving the estate of financier Stephen Jay Gould. He worked assiduously on that legal document, which the firm used at trial. Stotesbury himself expressed approval of Robeson's work on the brief.

The approval of the firm's head, however, was a rare exception in Robeson's work environment, which was ultimately one of pervasive racism. Robeson was the only African American in the entire office and almost everyone expressed hostility toward him. Accustomed to racial slights, he managed to tolerate the uncomfortable atmosphere until a dramatic incident pushed him to his limits. He had asked a legal secretary to take down a legal document. Instead of

fulfilling her employment obligations, she announced that she would not take dictation "from a nigger," and left the room. Robeson complained to Stotesbury, whose sympathy was genuine. Nevertheless, he candidly informed Robeson of the inherently limited prospects for a black lawyer in the racist professional environment of the 1920s. He explained that the firm's clients would probably feel uncomfortable with a black attorney appearing in court before white judges.

Stotesbury provided a career alternative to Paul Robeson. He proposed to open a Harlem branch of the firm, with Robeson in charge; this would provide some financial security and a base on which to launch a potential political career. But Robeson politely refused the offer. Instead, he resigned his position at the firm, concluding that he wanted no part of a profession where racism would restrict his options and progression so severely—a reality that has changed only marginally, when African Americans comprise only about 4 percent of the legal profession in the early twenty-first century. He never took the New York bar examination and abandoned his legal ambitions.

His decision troubled his wife Eslanda, who was concerned about his drift and lack of specific professional direction. But Paul Robeson actually aspired to enter the theater in a serious and more methodical way (the focus of Chapter Four). His abandonment of the law may have caused his wife some temporary distress, but that action ultimately catalyzed the start of his brilliant artistic odyssey that lasted until his retirement from public life. The law's loss was the world's gain.

Chapter 3:

PAUL ROBESON
THE ATHLETE

THE INTERNET AND OTHER informational sources are full of lists of great athletes. Among the top honorees from the past is Jim Thorpe, arguably the single-most talented athlete of all time. His gold-medal pentathlon and decathlon perform-ances in the 1912 Olympics, his collegiate and profes-sional football brilliance and his professional efforts in baseball and basketball made the Native American athlete a legend. Likewise included is Babe Didrickson Zaharias, whose stellar performances in golf, basketball and track and field, including the 1932 Olympics, earned her the reputation as the most talented female athlete of all time. Jackie Robinson also merits in-clusion, based on his remarkable feats as a varsity letter winner in baseball, football, basketball and track at UCLA and his Hall of Fame record as a Major League Baseball player. Robin-son is also well known and respected for being the first African American Major

League player of the modern era, and for his vigorous support of the civil rights movement following his baseball career.

Not surprisingly, Paul Robeson rarely appears on these lists of past greats, yet another legacy of his removal from American history. As recently as 1988, a routine sports news piece concerning Rutgers University football victories offered an intriguing observation: "Nestled in a turnpike wasteland is the site of the first college football game, where a mob of Rutgers men in 1869 first shed coats and vests and engaged in some lively shin-kicking and hair-mussing with Princeton. Rutgers contributed little of note in the sport since, until the Scarlet Knights upset two top 20 teams this season. . ."

This well-intentioned, witty story neglected the dramatic years of Paul Robeson's nationally visible exploits for the Rutgers football squad. Like most examples of daily journalism, little or no serious historical research informed the article. Readers would understandably assume that the 1988 effort was a unique departure from a long history of football mediocrity and invisibility. And they would scarcely be inclined to inquire more fully into the record, where they would find ample documentation about Robeson's football achievements. This is scarcely the first time that the national media, unintentionally, exacerbated Robeson's shameful exclusion from the historical record.

Exceptions to this sorry phenomenon exist, usually among African American scholars, journalists and athletes who have long recognized Robeson as one of the most accomplished and versatile athletes of the early twentieth century. The process of restoring Robeson's athletic reputation is a daunting task, because his artistic grandeur and his later, more controversial political activism eclipse his earlier record as a multitalented college and professional sports figure. This record deserves inclusion in any account of his life, both for its substance, and for his slow but inexorable res- urrection in the arena of athletic greatness.

Paul Robeson's earliest triumphs occurred at Somerville High School, where he starred on the football, basketball and baseball teams. By his senior year, he had grown to over six feet tall and weighed close to 200 pounds, giving him the powerful physical presence that augmented his stature in every feature of his life, even beyond athletics. On the gridiron, his dominance both on offense and defense attracted considerable statewide attention in New Jersey. Unfortunately, some of that attention reflected the racist resentment against a superior black athlete. Opponents, fearing his fierce play, especially his tackling, often retaliated, sometimes causing him injury, in accordance with the indifference of officials. In baseball, he played catcher and in basketball, he played center and forward. He also faced verbal racist assaults during his high-school sports activities. Because the coaching at Somerville High School was amateurish, he relied on his brother Ben's instruction, which enabled him to excel later at the collegiate level.

Robeson's legendary athletic accomplishments at Rutgers College began when he tried out for the football team. Coach Sanford knew of Robeson's talents, having seen him play at Somerville High. But the Rutgers college football veterans wanted no part in having a black teammate. Rutgers had never had a black player and many of the white players set out to prevent Robeson from making the team. At the first practice, they piled on young Robeson, leaving him with a broken nose, a sprained right shoulder and various cuts and bruises. He stayed in bed for ten days as a result of these injuries. He considered leaving Rutgers entirely and enrolling in his father's alma mater, Lincoln University, where he would no longer encounter such overwhelming white hostility.

Paul's brother Ben gave him a pep talk and encouraged him to return to practice. Robeson remembered that his father taught him never to be a quitter. At a subsequent practice, he lost his temper. Members of the varsity team came toward him, and he swept his massive arms out and brought down three men, grabbed the ball carrier and raised him over his head. As Robeson said, "I was going to smash him so hard to the ground that I'd break him right in two." Coach Sanford quickly intervened and said, "Robeson, you're on the varsity." He also told his players that anyone who tried to injure Paul would be dropped from the team.

Eventually, his white teammates accepted him, nicknaming him "Robey," and Coach Sanford taught him how to play football with precision and careful concentration, taking advantage of his prodigious natural talents. He worked hard on such football fundamentals as blocking, tackling and pass catching, and became a starter on the varsity during his freshman year. By the 1916 season, Robeson was a mainstay of the team. His performances on the field attracted major attention at the college, and the campus newspaper, the Targum, wrote glowing stories about his football prowess.

By 1917, his junior year, these exploits attracted wider journalistic attention, particularly in the major newspapers in nearby New York, including the *New York Sunday Tribune*, the *New York American*, the *New York Sun* and the *New York World*. Stories extolled his offensive and defensive attributes and frequently commented on his keen football instincts and intelligence. In both 1917 and 1918, Robeson was selected, in the position of offensive end, to be on Walter Camp's All-American team, one of the most singular honors of the sport. Camp, known as the "Father of American Football," called him a "veritable superman." By the end of the 1918 season, he had achieved national prominence and was widely regarded as one of the finest players in the land.

Unfortunately, like everything else at Rutgers, the specter of racism hovered over Robeson's efforts on the gridiron, including some incidents that had lifelong emotional significance. On road trips, he was compelled to live apart from his teammates and sometimes had to take his meals on the team bus. He constantly faced excessive violence from members of other teams, although he had learned how to defend himself effectively. Often, football officials on the field, many of whom were southerners, looked the other way when rival teammates assaulted Robeson. Racial slurs, including "nigger," were commonplace from crowds in the stands.

Some southern opponents like William and Mary and Georgia Tech even refused to play against a team with a black player. The worst insult occurred when Washington and Lee of Lexington, Virginia was scheduled to play Rutgers in New Brunswick for its 150th anniversary. Rutgers officials were anxious to keep the festivities calm and orderly, probably to attract alumni contributions. When Washington and Lee demanded that Paul Robeson be kept off the playing field because of his race, the Rutgers administration complied, viewing it as a "courtesy" to the other team, a convenient rhetorical veil for racism.

Although some Rutgers players protested the decision to bench Robeson for this game, the Rutgers policy prevailed. Paul Robeson was unable to resort to his usual mechanism of pretending that he had another engagement elsewhere. He merely sat on the bench with the substitutes for the entire game, which ended in a 13-13 tie score. It is impossible to know what went through his mind during the game, but it is likely that he felt an enormous sense of humiliation. His close friend and collaborator, Lloyd Brown, in *The Young Paul Robeson*, noted that he never liked hearing about that incident, which generated a lifelong ambivalence that he felt about his alma mater. As Robeson later told Brown, a more politically savvy and mature version of himself would have refused to play again for Rutgers in order to be true to himself. Of course, such an action in 1916 would also have meant that he would never have achieved the football glory that made him the legendary, "Robeson of Rutgers."

Robeson's athletic greatness wasn't exclusive to his Rutgers football record. During his undergraduate years, he won fifteen varsity letters in four different sports, reinforcing his status as one of most versatile athletes in American history. He played center and forward on the college basketball team (and was the leading scorer), catcher on the baseball team, and he threw the discus, javelin and shot put on the track team. Reflecting his remarkable versatility, on one day in May 1918, he competed in a collegiate baseball game and walked to an adjoining field to participate in the shot put and javelin competition, and then returned to his baseball responsibilities.

Although his performances in the other sports never rose to the level of his football brilliance, he had one emotionally gratifying success on the baseball diamond at the end of his Rutgers studies. On the very afternoon of his valedictorian speech, Robeson took the field as the catcher against the hated team from Princeton University—a school that had defeated Rutgers in every contest of every sport for many years. Rutgers won the final game 5-1 in Robeson's last appearance in a Rutgers uniform. Defeating Rutgers's rival would have been a source of jubilation in itself, but Robeson also savored that final baseball victory because of Princeton's strongly deserved racist reputation, having denied admission to many qualified black students. Robeson, understandably, could not forget his role as a proud black American.

Paul Robeson extended his athletic legacy during his studies at Columbia Law School. He entered professional football through his association with Fritz Pollard, another black All-American football player who had performed spectacularly at Brown University. Robeson worked part time for Pollard as assistant football coach at Lincoln University, and when Pollard was invited to play pro football, he brought Robeson along with him. In 1920, they joined the Akron

Pros, a team in a fledgling league that later became the National Football League. Surprisingly, blacks were permitted to play professional football until owners banned them at the start of the 1934 season.

Pay ranged from $50 to over $500 per game, allowing Robeson to pay his law school and living expenses. Games were played on Sundays, requiring complex travel arrangements to make practice sessions on the Saturday before the game day. He took the train from New York to Philadelphia and joined Pollard and then traveled through the night to any of the cities where the game was scheduled: Buffalo, Chicago, Columbus, Canton, Rochester, Cleveland and several others. After the game, he journeyed back to New York to resume his law classes.

In his first professional season, Robeson's Akron squad won every game. After a second season with Akron, the team was somewhat less successful, with a 7-2-1 record, finishing third in the league. Despite the overall success of the Akron Pros, the same racism that Robeson encountered as a Rutgers football star was present in Akron, Ohio. Chants and racial slurs were common. Denial of service at restaurants and hotels also reflected the dominant racial discrimination of the era, in the North as well as the South.

For the 1922 season, Pollard and Robeson joined the Milwaukee Badgers. Although the team as a whole was mediocre, Robeson was able to recapture some of his collegiate glory. His most famous game for the Badgers took place on November 19, 1922, when the team played the Marion, Ohio Indians, led by the legendary Jim Thorpe. Before a crowd of eight thousand, Robeson led his team to a 13-0 victory, scoring both touchdowns. Thorpe himself revealed flashes of his football brilliance in a losing effort. Above all, this was a rare opportunity to see, in one contest, two of America's finest multi-sport athletes compete against one another.

Robeson dabbled further in basketball as a Rutgers undergraduate. While starting at Rutgers, he also played center and forward for the club basketball team for St. Christopher in Harlem, which he continued while he studied at Columbia Law School. As a law student, he picked up small amounts of money playing semi-pro basketball in the New York area.

Although a minor feature of his overall athletic record, his basketball efforts reveal a fuller picture of his multifaceted athleticism.

Despite his brilliant record, the same forces that succeeded in obscuring Robeson from national history and public consciousness also erased him from the annals of American sports history. In a particularly egregious example, the 1951 edition of the *College Football and All America Review* listed a ten-man All-American team for 1918, leaving out the name of Paul Robeson. The omission reflected the deep fear and anti-communist hysteria of the times, but the educational consequences of such censorship are long lasting. The protracted struggle to induct Robeson into the College Football Hall of Fame was equally as troublesome. His candidacy had been put forward in 1970, but his long overdue recognition in 1995 occurred only after a deliberate campaign by Robeson supporters (and sportswriters committed to athletic excellence) to correct a grievous historical omission. For decades, Robeson was denied induction solely because of his unpopular political record.

Slowly but inexorably, the full restoration of Paul Robeson's reputation will encompass his stature as a world-class athlete. But that knowledge alone, however valuable, is insufficient. Sociologist Harry Edwards, in his perceptive 1978 essay, "Paul Robeson: His Political Legacy for the Twentieth-Century Gladiator," urged African American athletes to transcend their roles as mere gladiators in the service of capitalist America. He implored them to accept the burdens of social responsibility for their people and for humanity in general. He championed such stalwart African American athletes as Jackie Robinson, Tommie Smith, John Carlos and Muhammad Ali for their highly publicized, often unpopular efforts in standing up for their principles and using their athletic fame on behalf of deeper social and moral goals. As Edwards perceptively writes, long before any of these courageous figures, "there stood Paul Robeson."

Chapter 4:

PAUL ROBESON
THE STAGE
ACTOR

PAUL ROBESON'S FUTURE AS A PERFORMING ARTIST BEGAN while he was a law student. The young woman who became his wife, Eslanda Cardoza Goode (known to many as Essie), eventually became the manager of his artistic career in stage, film and singing. Another of Robeson's friends, Dora Cole Norman, persuaded him to participate in an amateur theatrical production in Harlem while he was in law school, creating the foundation for his thirty-five-year acting career.

In the 1920s, abandoning his intended profession as a lawyer, he also embarked on his film and singing efforts, propelling him to international attention and acclaim. His tripartite reputation as a performing artist also enabled him, in due course, to have a wide forum for the social and political views that increasingly defined his overall identity.

Dora Cole Norman was the producer of white playwright Ridgeley Torrence's *Simon the Cyrenian*, a production at the Harlem YWCA. This 1920 effort was the story of the black man who bore the cross for Jesus to Golgotha. Robeson was initially reluctant to participate, but Mrs. Norman, impressed by his striking physical presence and his powerful speaking voice, prevailed on him to undertake the leading role of Simon. At the time, he had not considered the theater as a professional option, even though some influential theatrical personas who had witnessed his performance were impressed by what they had seen.

In March 1922, however, the lure of acting returned, and once again, Dora Cole Norman played a major role. Robeson had completed another professional football season and was looking to earn some money. She prodded him to try out for his first professional role in a play entitled *Taboo*, by another white playwright, Mary Hoyt Wiborg. The obscure, melodramatic plot involved a plantation in Louisiana. Paul Robeson was selected to play the role of the wandering minstrel Jim. He worked hard during re-hearsals learning his lines and honing his dramatic skills. Critics, however, panned the play, which lasted only four matinee performances. Reviewers were generally impressed with Robeson, except for the *New York Times* critic, who wrote that he belonged anywhere but in the theater. But his wife Eslanda was sufficiently impressed, and she began encouraging him to consider acting as an alternative or supplement to a legal career.

Robeson and Eslanda went regularly to the theater, where he reflected on the actors' performances. Slowly, his interest in dramatic techniques grew, as a return to stage acting ap-peared attractive, even beyond serving as a convenient source of income. The opportunity soon emerged when Robeson joined the cast of the musical *Shuffle Along* in May

1922, an all-black cast in a minstrel-like effort where he sang "Old Black Joe" while wearing a straw hat and carrying a cane. Although he must have blanched at the racial stereotypes of *Shuffle Along*, Robeson used his role in the performance to augment his theatrical development.

That role led to an invitation to star in a summer production of *Taboo* in England, renamed *Voodoo* for its British debut. Robeson accepted unhesitatingly, postponing his plans to take summer law courses at Columbia, but assured that he could return to enroll in the fall term and continue as a professional football player after the English performance. He sailed for England in July 1922, and began rehearsing after his arrival, unaware that Eslanda was hospitalized resulting from complications from an earlier appendectomy. The play opened in Blackpool, and was received poorly by audiences and critics. When *Voodoo* opened in Edinburgh later in July, however, the reception was much more favorable. Audiences were enthusiastic about Robeson's performance, which would also be well received during its run in Glasgow. His strength alone, however, could not save the effort as a whole.

Robeson's time abroad left an impression on him; he felt at ease, impelling his frequent return to England, Scotland and Wales throughout his life. In London, he made the fortuitous acquaintance of American musician Lawrence Brown, who was working as an accompanist for notable African American concert singer Roland Hayes. The two were drawn together by Brown's interests in Robeson's voice, and Robeson's interest in Brown's knowledge of American Negro spirituals and folk music. Later, the two men would collaborate for many years, adding luster to musical history in the process.

Eslanda finally cabled him about her recuperation from her surgery, and Robeson immediately returned to the United States. He stayed with her constantly during her recovery and then enrolled in his final year in both law school and pro football. Following the regrettable period in the Stotesbury law firm, and after drifting a bit, Robeson concluded that a serious dramatic career would best suit his interests and temperament. Earlier in 1923, he had corresponded with Eugene O'Neill, who invited him to stay in touch.

Soon afterwards, Robeson received a message from the director of the Provincetown Players, inviting him to audition for the lead part in O'Neill's *All God's Chillun Got Wings,* a play about the delicate topic of interracial marriage. He got the part, impressing the Provincetown selectors with his powerful presence, personality and voice—the same qualities that pervaded every feature of his artistic life and political activism for decades to come. A series of delays for the opening of *All God's Chillun Got Wings* allowed him to increase his singing engagements (see Chapter Six) and perform in other brief theatrical endeavors. He also used the time to make major contacts in the African American cultural and political communities. All of this increased his visibility and generated excitement about his forthcoming role in the O'Neill production.

One of his brief theatrical roles was another of Eugene O'Neill's plays, *The Emperor Jones,* requiring herculean effort to prepare for two major dramatic efforts. With his wife's methodical assistance, he managed the preparation and performed outstandingly, with O'Neill in at the opening. Reviews were exemplary, one even comparing him to the legendary African American actor Charles Gilpin, who had made the play famous. Robeson was well underway to his professional success as a stage actor.

The opening of *Chillun* in May 1924 came after considerable controversy and threats from the Ku Klux Klan and other racist elements protesting a scene with Jim, the black lawyer played by Paul Robeson, kissing his white wife—a daring, even taboo theme at the time. No protests or disruptions occurred. Reviews were mixed, except for accolades on Robeson's performance. His success enabled his wife to formally undertake the role as his artistic manger, soon arranging for the start of his film career in Oscar Micheaux's *Body and Soul* (see Chapter Five), and made Paul Robeson a growing presence in the burgeoning Harlem Renaissance, along with writers, musicians, political figures and other black luminaries.

By January 1925, Eslanda Robeson had concluded an arrangement for her husband to perform in an English production of *The Emperor Jones*. In August, they sailed to England where he performed again to excellent personal reviews despite mixed reactions to the play itself. Robeson and Eslanda found England extremely congenial, meeting numerous people and enjoying a full social calendar.

Returning to the United States, Paul Robeson pursued his singing career more methodically. But the stage was always a major focus and in August 1926 he began rehearsing for *Black Boy*, based on the tumultuous life of controversial black prizefighter Jack Johnson, co-starring Fredi Washington. As before, Robeson's reviews were better than reviews for the play itself, which closed after a few weeks. He returned to the concert stage once again.

But his greatest dramatic triumphs still lay ahead. On November 2, 1927, Eslanda gave birth to Paul Robeson, Jr. in a difficult delivery while her husband was in Europe on a concert tour. After a protracted recovery, she resumed her role as his agent. Robeson received an offer from Florenz Ziegfield to sing in *Show Boat* in London. The play had been a huge success on Broadway and ran for close to a year at London's famous Drury Lane Theater. The story deals with the lives of black and white people involved with a Mississippi River showboat from 1880 to 1927. British audiences packed the theater and were thrilled by Robeson's rendition of "Ol' Man River," the highlight of the show, which became Paul Robeson's signature song. The London press gave his performance rave reviews, although as before, his reviews were superior to those of the play in general. This reception made him an extremely popular star and further augmented his growing reputation as a vocalist in England by the end of the 1920s. *Show Boat* was also a strong financial success, adding to Robeson's marketability as a stage actor and providing him with a handsome salary for his performance.

Some critics in the black press in the United States, however, had more critical reactions to Robeson's portrayal of Joe the River man in the play. Lyrics commonly used racial slurs ("Niggers all work on the Mississippi"), which Robeson himself changed throughout his concert performances and recordings in future years, and blacks were casually reinforced as being lazy and good-natured. Many blacks saw his performance as merely confirming white attitudes about African Americans. Robeson did perform his role with extraordinary pathos and dignity, revealing the pain of racism, but it remained an open question whether those qualities were sufficient to overcome the perpetuation of racial stereotypes in the 1928 performance on the London stage.

The success of *Show Boat* encouraged Robeson and Eslanda to remain in London, leaving son Paul, Jr. with Eslanda's mother. They found England more congenial, with much less overt racism than they had encountered in America. In London, they also met several new acquaintances. Among them were leftist members of the Labor Party, and key figures of the British cultural elite, many of whom, like H.G. Wells and George Bernard Shaw, helped Robeson form the social and political views that would eventually pervade his art and his life.

The closing of *Show Boat* in February 1929 gave rise to what would become Paul Robeson's greatest and most memorable performance as a dramatic actor: the role of the

Moor in Shakespeare's *Othello*. No black actor had starred in this classic tragedy since the iconic Ira Aldrige played the role in the nineteenth century. Robeson prepared meticulously for the role. He read Shakespeare and studied the language of his time. The production was organized by Maurice Browne and his wife, Ellen Van Volkenbeg, who assembled a talented cast, including Peggy Ashcroft as Desdemona and Browne as Iago.

The reviews were generally positive, including Robeson's performance, but some critics also noted some technical deficiencies in his role, which he would improve later in his reprise of *Othello* on the New York stage in 1943. In 1930, Robeson had yet to develop the confidence he later demonstrated as a Shakespearean actor, but his commanding presence and his careful preparation carried the day with his audiences. In his first English performance of *Othello*, Robeson's vision of the play was less specifically racial than the way it eventually evolved. That latter vision would fundamentally alter public perception of Shakespeare's great drama and encourage readers and viewers alike to consider the play in context of the great racial upheavals and controversies in Robeson's native land.

Robeson was committed to bringing his performance of *Othello* to the United States, but his other commitments and the strong sentiments against mixed racial casting in America delayed him for more than a dozen years. This goal did eventually materialize. It made way for Robeson's greatest role on Broadway, and augmented his world stature as a performing artist. The experienced Shakespearean director Margaret Webster cast the play with Jose

Scene from "Othello" with Paul Robeson as Othello and Uta Hagen as Desdemona, Theatre Guild Production, Broadway, 1943-44

Ferrer as Iago and Uta Hagen as Desdemona. Testing the run initially in Cambridge, Princeton, New Haven and Boston before its Broadway debut on October 19, 1943, the effort was groundbreaking; a black actor kissing a white actress on a Broadway stage was considered so provocative that it inevitably generated extreme public controversy.

The racial tension of that era was powerful, revealing the depth of racism in the not-so-distant past. *Life* magazine published a pictorial story about Robeson's *Othello* performance, attracting several racist comments from readers. One such comment from South Carolina claimed that, "[s]uch pictures have a tendency to create in negroes a longing for something that cannot be theirs and can only lead to a feeling of frustration." Nevertheless, the 1943 performance was extraordinarily well received among audiences and critics alike. Although a few reviewers continued to express some doubts about his performance, the consensus was that Paul Robeson had become a modern master in his role, with a majestic quality rarely seen on the American or British stage. Equally important, his effort broke the racial barricade holding that audiences for *Othello* would refuse to accept a black actor in the leading role, and that they preferred instead to see white actors with artificially darkened faces. Since Robeson's groundbreaking performance, major African American actors such as Earle Hyman, William Marshall, Paul Winfield, Yaphet Kotto, James Earl Jones, Lawrence Fishburne, Avery Brooks and others have appeared as the tragic Moor.

Robeson's Othello set a Broadway record that still stands: 296 performances that lasted from 1943 to 1945, at the height of his power and popularity. By then, he had become acutely involved in the struggles of African Americans for freedom and dignity in their own land. That perspective was reflected in his understanding and interpretation of Shakespeare's tragedy. In a 1943 interview, he noted that Shakespeare posed the problem of a black man in a white society in *Othello*. He understood Othello as a strong black man operating in a hostile white society, where powerful forces conspired to bring him down. Robeson saw the problem of the character of Othello as the problem of his own people and as a tragedy of racial conflict as well as a portrayal of the more universal themes of love, jealousy, pride and honor. He invited audiences to politicize the drama as a racial inquiry, offering the opportunity to examine the Moor's downfall in the context of contemporary racial issues—a view that is no less relevant in the early twenty-first century than it was in 1943. Although many scholars and critics continue to be unnerved by the infusion of politics into art, Robeson's vision helped create the foundation for a much wider appreciation for the connectedness of art and politics within every creative medium.

Following the Broadway performance, *Othello* toured the United States and Canada for nine months. The show regularly sold out its seats, and encompassed over fourteen thousand miles and forty-five cities, with the exclusion of the segregated South. Approximately a half a million people saw the play, including large numbers of people who did not regularly attend live theater. These included union members and African Americans who knew Robeson primarily for his singing or film roles. Responses were generally excellent; his performance as well as those of Uta Hagen and Jose Ferrer often thrilled audiences unable to see Robeson as Othello on Broadway. Critical reviews were also excellent, reinforcing Robeson's reputation as one of the most powerful modern interpreters of this role. The tour concluded with a two-week run in New York in June 1945 to highly appreciative audiences.

The 1943 to 1945 *Othello* run was a highlight for American theater and racial history. It was also the apex of Paul Robeson's career as a stage actor, bringing him enormous public acclaim and numerous awards, including the prestigious Springarn Medal from the National Association for the Advancement of Colored People in 1945. It also increased his public visibility as a spokesperson for African Americans and for the political causes that increasingly became the dominant focus of his life.

In 1959, Robeson played Othello for the final time in Stratford-upon-Avon, England. Having recently recovered his passport after years of US State Department denial and the debilitating blacklist, and despite his declining health, Robeson prepared for a very different version of the play. Director Tony Richardson organized an entirely untraditional production, featuring a fireworks display, dogs running across the stage and other elements that conflicted with Paul Robson's image of dignity and nobility. The production ran for seven months and Robeson never missed a single performance during that time. The play constantly showed to sold out audiences and Robeson received considerably higher acclaim than did the production as a whole. Once again, his powerful presence and his majestic voice carried the day, enabling him a final dramatic triumph before the disabilities of physical and mental health forced him from the public arena.

Othello was the only Shakespearean role of Robeson's career as a stage actor. Between his performances as the tragic Moor, he also performed in other significant dramatic efforts. In 1931, for example, he appeared in another Eugene O'Neill play, *The Hairy Ape,* which received strong reviews but which also closed after only five performances in London. The immediate cause was laryngitis, but it also probably reflected his continuing marital difficulties with Eslanda, and could have been an early sign of the depression that debilitated him many decades later.

Robeson also appeared in Andre Van Gyseghem's *Stevedore* in 1935, a London production that addressed the issues of race and class, allowing Robeson to promote his developing vision of progressive artistic content. The cast consisted mostly of nonprofessional actors and told the story of a black worker falsely accused of raping a white woman—an all-too-typical scenario in the United States, often leading to lynching and various judicial injustices. In the play, the central protagonist, played by Robeson, rallied other blacks, and white union members, to repel a rioting lynch mob.

In March 1936, Robeson played the lead role in two London performances of *Toussaint L'Ouverture* by C. L. R. James, the renowned Afro-Trinidadian scholar and leftist theorist. This dramatic effort concerned the leader of the Haitian slave revolt and revolution against France, which resulted in the first independent black state in the Western hemisphere. Audiences responded enthusiastically to Robeson's portrayal of the heroic figure, but the play was unable to attract sufficient financial support to continue its run.

In June 1938, Robeson performed in *Plant in the Sun*, by American writer Ben Bengal, directed by Herbert Marshall, which Unity Theater staged in London. He had helped establish this group as a workers' theater for the British trade union movement, and he was attracted to the play because its pro-union focus reflected his political sentiments. Moreover, he played an Irishman, the first time he had performed a "white" role in a dramatic effort. The month-long run attracted sold-out audiences and excellent reviews. Robeson performed the role without fee and the other cast members were all amateur actors, with whom he established warm rapport.

Yet another example of personal glory in a critical and financial failure occurred in 1939 and 1940 when Robeson starred in *John Henry* by Raork Bradford. This musical was based on its namesake, the black railroad worker and legendary folk hero. The role was consistent with Robeson's vision about the need for positive imagery for his people. The initial cast included talented African American folksinger and civil rights activist Josh White and a young member of the chorus, Bayard Rustin, later to become one of the most effective civil rights organizers and activists in American history. But the play bombed in its initial performances in Philadelphia and Boston and lasted only seven performances on Broadway. Critics dismissed the play, but hailed Robeson's acting and singing.

Beyond his stellar contributions on the stage, Paul Robeson helped pave the way for generations of younger black actors, many of who have acknowledged his profound influence as a powerful forerunner and role model. As in so many of his activities, he was a trailblazer of the highest order. In his 2011 memoir *My Song*, another remarkable actor, singer and activist, Harry Belafonte, summed up Paul Robeson's impact concisely and eloquently:

> **"In all I'd done, he'd guided and inspired me. My whole life was an homage to him."**

Chapter 5:
PAUL ROBESON THE SCREEN ACTOR

AUDIENCES THROUGHOUT THE WORLD ARE ACCUSTOMED to routinely seeing black male film stars. Contemporary figures like Denzel Washington, Lawrence Fishburne, Jamie Foxx, Morgan Freeman, Forest Whitaker, Eddie Murphy, Samuel L. Jackson, Don Cheadle, Cuba Gooding, Blair Underwood, Will Smith and scores of others owe their successes and reputations to such earlier icons as Eddie Anderson, Ossie Davis, Sidney Poitier, Harry Belafonte, James Earl Jones, Brock Peters and others who blazed the path, not always easily, in a film industry remarkably resistant to providing blacks roles that reflect dignity and respect on people of African heritage. But even before those giants, there stood Paul Robeson, one of the earliest black stars in American and British cinema history, another manifestation of his colossal status as an artistic, athletic and political pioneer and trailblazer.

From 1924 until 1942, Robeson had major roles in eleven motion pictures, increasing his visibility to audiences throughout the United States and Europe. His entry into the film industry placed him directly into an arena with a history of portraying black people in demeaning and degrading ways. Its treatment of African Americans in the early twentieth century was remarkably similar to the racist context of Robeson's early life. The most egregious example was D. W. Griffith's 1915 "classic," *Birth of a Nation.* This film highlighted a vision of post-Civil War black savagery and glorified the Ku Klux Klan, offering cinematic reinforcement to the prevailing white racism of the times. It reflected a film industry that showed little or no sensitivity to the basic humanity of millions of black Americans.

In her pictorial biography of her grandfather, *The Whole World in His Hands*, Susan Robeson offers a perspective on Paul Robeson's basic aims in becoming a film actor. She suggests that his,

> "journey through the world of cinema was a search to express the inner cultural core of Black people."

Above all, she notes, he understood the medium of film as something that transcended simple entertainment; rather, he believed it should be a force to imbue people of African heritage with dignity and pride, and reveal their strength and intelligence in a growing medium of mass communication.

There is little doubt that Robeson wanted his roles to reflect a strong and positive vision of his people, especially as he grew increasingly conscious of his social and ethical responsibilities as a public screen artist. To a limited extent, at least in some of his films, he succeeded. At other times, he performed exceptionally well in films where he had little or no control over the final product and where the works both reflected and reinforced major racist images of black people in America and Africa. Sometimes his talents were exploited in order to demean the black race even further. Critics in the African American community and elsewhere applauded his role as a pioneering black film actor, even as they decried the stereotypical roles he was asked to perform on screen. At the end of his film career in 1942, and at the height of his artistic prowess and fame, he came to concur with that critique.

Robeson began his film career in 1924 in one of his two silent efforts, *Body and Soul*. Eslanda Robeson concluded arrangements with director Oscar Micheaux, the premier African American filmmaker of the era. Paul played a double role, as a corrupt, dissolute pastor and his sincere, virtuous brother. His performance was strong and charismatic; it reflected the same impressive physical presence he brought to the stage, but as a silent film, which means it lacked his greatest asset, his majestic voice. The film's reception, however, was problematic. Its plot was confusing and many in the black community found its portrayal of a depraved clergyman offensive. It also had little or no crossover appeal, and Robeson never realized the financial gains that his wife had hoped for in the contract with Micheaux.

His next film, six years later, titled *Borderline*, proved to be the oddest production of his career as a film actor. Director Kenneth Macpherson filmed this experimental silent work in Switzerland, with Robeson as the lead and his wife Eslanda playing his cinematic wife. The plot was set in a border town somewhere in Europe where a white couple and a black couple cross paths, inciting racial and interpersonal conflicts. But the plot, like that in *Body and Soul*, was confusing. The director was much more interested in experimental film techniques than in content. While the Robesons enjoyed their brief continental stay during the filming, the work itself had little critical or financial success and is still regarded as a curious divergent in Robeson's overall work in film.

His major exposure in the field came a few years later, after his London debut in *Othello*. The 1933 film version of *The Emperor Jones* was his first major commercial movie. One of his best-known films, this effort propelled him to the forefront of African American cinematic history. Robeson received $15,000 plus expenses for six weeks of filming in a Long Island studio, and his contract provided that he would not be required to shoot footage south of the Mason-Dixon line.

The Dudley Murphy directed film follows the plotline of the Eugene O'Neill play. Robeson portrays Brutus Jones, a strong black man who refuses to bow to anyone. As a Pullman porter, even when he is deferential to his white employers and passengers, his strength of character reveals him to be a man of powerful self-confidence. When he kills another black man in a crap game, he is arrested and sentenced to a chain gang. As in some of his other films, the setting allowed Robeson to display his magnificent singing voice in a stirring rendition of "Water Boy." After witnessing the brutal treatment of black prisoners, Brutus Jones escapes and with the help of his wife, hops on a freighter to the Caribbean.

There, the tyrannical black ruler captures him. In chorus with a white trader named Smithers, he overthrows the dictator and assumes power himself, as the "Emperor Jones." But he soon exceeds the previous dictator's cruelty, falling into the total corruption of political power. At the end, his subjects, under the leadership of the white man Smithers, capture and kill the bare-chested (a provocative and daring sight at the time), psychologically deranged Emperor Jones.

This film was typical of the mixed messages delivered to the large African American audiences who saw it. Many black viewers were delighted to see a black film star, especially with the powerful presence of Paul Robeson. They and some black film critics likewise appreciated seeing a black role where, for most of the narrative, whites were in a subordinate position. Brutus Jones dramatically, for example, resists the white prison guards as he makes his escape. He also takes power on his own, if somewhat illegitimately. His sneering remarks to Smithers even reveal a glimpse of black militancy in the plot.

The theme of the ultimate corruption of power transcends race; neither white nor black tyrants are immune from its excesses. Nevertheless, the film also highlights several racist images of African Americans. Its depiction of the irresponsible, gambling and womanizing Jones amidst other cartoonish black characters only reinforced dominant white perceptions of the black population in the United States. The final victory of the white trader over Emperor Jones also underscored the true nature of racial power. The result is ambiguous, not unlike Paul Robeson's entire cinematic journey.

Robeson appeared in a British production for his next film in 1935. Having begun his explorations of Africa, he wanted a film opportunity that would reflect his identification with Africa and enable audiences to understand African cultural roots. He accepted an offer to play the lead role of Bosambo in *Sanders of the River*, directed by Zoltan Korda. His hope was to portray a strong African figure with dignity and provide a broader view of African culture to Western audiences. His initial optimism about the role was informed by Korda's preparatory documentary footage in Central Africa, which recorded significant features of music, dance and other rituals. As the filming proceeded in the summer of 1934 outside London, hundreds of black extras were used, including anti-colonialist activist Jomo Kenyatta, later the liberation leader of Kenya. Robeson was encouraged that scenes appeared to be authentic reconstructions of actual African settings.

The final edited version of *Sanders of the River*, however, was nothing like Robeson imagined. Instead, the film was little more than a celebration of British imperialism. Bosambo had been transformed into a loyal minion of his British superiors—a cinematic justification of British rule in Africa. Black Africans, as usual in the entertainment industry, were depicted as childish savages totally dependent on the civilized influence of their white masters. It would not be the last time that Paul Robeson would be discouraged by his film roles in the mainstream film industry.

In 1935, Robeson starred in his first film for a major Hollywood studio. *Show Boat*, the film version of the original stage musical, enabled him to recreate the role of Joe, for a substantial fee. The highlight of the film was when he sang

Jerome Kern and Oscar Hammerstein's "Ol' Man River," which helped to establish him as a major film star and reinforce his strong reputation as a concert singer. This segment of *Show Boat*—widely available on the Internet nearly a half a century later—showcased his vocal talents reinforcing "Ol' Man River" as Paul Robeson's most famous song. The movie was generally well received, largely because of Robeson's performance, even among black critics, although some continued to comment on the stereotypical role that he played in the film.

Back in England, he still sought film roles that would express a more respectful vision of Africa and its people. In 1936, he starred in *Song of Freedom*, a substantial improvement from *Sanders of the River*. Starring opposite Elizabeth Welch and directed by Elder Wills, he played Zinga, a black dockworker in London with a magnificent singing voice. In the storyline, an opera producer discovers him fortuitously, and leads him to an international concert stage career. Zinga learns that he is descended from African royalty and abandons his lucrative career to return with his wife to his African homeland, seeking to merge the best of Western technology and medicine with traditional African culture. Both Zinga and his wife are intelligent people with thoughtful and admirable, if somewhat utopian, ambitions.

The final impact of *Song of Freedom* is more complex than many of his other films. Never a commercial success, it allowed Robeson to highlight strong black African-British characters—rare in film history at the time. But the movie also extensively depicted Africans as the "savage natives" that the Tarzan movies of the 1930s and 1940s showcased so pervasively. This aspect of *Song of Freedom* contradicted Robeson's individual performance and diminished a more sympathetic and realistic understanding of Africa and its peoples.

King Solomon's Mines, another British film from 1937, also used an African setting. Here, Robeson once again played a displaced African chief, Umbopa, in a lavish production that used African documentary footage and numerous extras. Characteristic of the era, the storyline was trite: Umbopa, a servant, reveals his true identity and regains his power. He proceeds to save the lives of the treasure-seeking whites. Above all, the film featured Robeson's singing, even while portraying African "natives" in absurd garb and behaving in the usual stereotypical ways. The major difference between this production and the earlier *Sanders of the River* was simply that it had no overt promotion of western imperialism. Still, the production, while again highlighting Robeson's magnificent voice, scarcely reflected his growing political consciousness and his deepening commitment to authentic African culture.

Still from Paul Robeson in "Sanders of The River

Another British film in 1937, *Jericho*, gave Robeson the opportunity to play a more forceful character, although this film also had familiar features of black stereotypes and racial subordination. Filmed in Egypt, it enabled him and his wife to spend time in Cairo and experience North African culture. Robeson played Jericho Jackson, an American medical student drafted in an all black unit (commanded by white officers) in World War I. On the troop ship, Jackson, defying a direct order, saves trapped men from below the deck after the ship is torpedoed. In the process, he accidentally kills a white superior and faces a court martial. He escapes his death sentence and flees to North Africa, where he marries the daughter of a Tuareg chief. He uses his medical knowledge to help the people and their chief, and then leads the group on the annual trek for their supply of salt. In the process, he displays his military acumen with his heroism in battle. Meanwhile, the disgraced US Army captain who let Jericho escape sees him in a documentary on the "Great Salt Trek" and vows to recapture him. The ending finds a guilt-stricken Jericho leaving on a plane with his commanding officer to return to clear the captain's name.

Jericho Jackson is a highly educated and inspirational leader—a major departure from conventional depictions of African European, and American blacks. His bold escape from an unjust trial and sentence and his medical assistance to his adopted tribe reveal his resolve to live an authentic and autonomous life. Nevertheless, at various points in *Jericho,* Robeson breaks incongruously into song, highlighting his prodigious talent but weakening the film narrative. The most disconcerting feature of the movie are his fellow soldiers, many of whom are shown as ludicrous clowns and cowards, as bad as the worst racist caricatures of the era. Moreover, Jericho's extreme deference to his white captain in the end reinforces the racial structure of power, with its familiar scheme of white superiority and black inferiority. Although *Jericho* is more positive in its depiction of black people compared with many of Robeson's other roles, it remains fundamentally limited by the deeper racism of its times.

His effort a year later in 1938, *Big Fella,* reprised the same team as *Song of Freedom*: director Elder Wills and co-star Elizabeth Welch. It also included his wife Eslanda and his longtime musical accompanist Larry Brown in small supporting roles. Based on Claude McKay's novel *Banjo,* Robeson played a dockworker who, as usual in Robeson's films, regularly sang in the midst of the film narrative. He finds a lost boy and helps his family raise him, but eventually returns to the docks. Although the movie wasn't particularly remarkable, the role allowed Robeson to play an ordinary black male who functioned effectively in a white, British society. This unique angle made it qualitatively different from most of his other efforts in his film career.

In 1939, Robeson agreed to star in a film that he subsequently regarded as his best effort artistically and politically. Director Pen Tennyson filmed *Proud Valley* on location in Welsh coal mining country. Robeson played David Goliath, a black American miner who shares the daily lives and challenges of his fellow workers. Goliath wins the trust and respect of the workers through his magnificent voice as a member of the workers' choir. His true nature emerges at the end of the film when he sacrifices his own life while saving fellow miners during an accident. *Proud Valley* reveals the harsh conditions of Welsh mineworkers, and depicts Robeson's character as an authentic black hero (even though a black man loses his life while the white miners retain theirs). This action, representing black strength and courage, is the antithesis of the usual portrayals in the British and American film industries and historically throughout popular culture.

Paul Robeson's final film, *Tales of Manhattan*, in 1942 catalyzed his decision to abandon film, only one element of his three-part artistic career at the time. Roberson had become world renowned as a singer, dramatic actor, and film star. *Tales of Manhattan* was a Hollywood production with some of the biggest stars of the times, including Charles Boyer, Rita Hayworth, Ginger Rogers, Henry Fonda, Charles Laughton, Edward G. Robinson, Cesar Romero and others. It also included two other African Americans besides Robeson, Ethel Waters and Eddie "Rochester" Anderson. The movie consisted of five marginally connected stories and, to Robeson's regret, reinforced traditional stereotypes of black childishness and clownish behavior in relation to whites.

Although the film marginally exposed the deplorable conditions of blacks' lives under the southern sharecropping system, many black critics and reviewers were critical, even hostile, to *Tales of Manhattan*. Robeson had objected to some of the derogatory images of his people at the script stage, but was unable to do anything about them—a reality quite typical of his entire film career. The final result so disturbed him that he said he would join those who would picket the film because they found it racially offensive. He denounced Hollywood's "plantation" attitude towards blacks and announced his decision to refrain from making any more films for major studios, effectively ending his eighteen-year run as a major film actor.

One final film effort in 1942 caught Robeson's attention. Eschewing big-budget Hollywood productions in favor of the alternative politically progressive cinema, he narrated and sang in the feature-length documentary *Native Land*. Directed by Leo Hurwitz and Paul Strand, both leftists, and with a musical score by Marc Blitzstein, the film promoted a pro-union, antifascist message that reflected Robeson's political posture at the time. The film reflected the findings of the LaFollette Senate Committee in 1938 that documented egregious civil-liberty violations against union organizing. Robeson accepted the minimum fee that the union allowed, and promptly donated it to Frontier Films, the producer of *Native Land*.

CONSISTENTLY

DIRECTORS FORCED PAUL INTO DEMEANING ROLES

AS HE LAMENTED, "THE BIG PRODUCERS INSISTED ON PRESENTING A CARICATURE IMAGE OF THE BLACK, A RIDICULOUS IMAGE, THAT AMUSES THE WHITE BOURGEOISIE AND I AM NOT INTERESTED IN PLAYING THEIR GAME"

Overall, Paul Robeson left a positive but still ambiguous legacy as a film actor. Despite the many demeaning roles he played, he managed to use his growing international stature to obtain employment for many black actors, even in minor roles as extras. He also used his films to showcase his remarkable singing ability, advancing his career as a concert and recording artist. Above all, as African American film scholar Donald Bogle noted, what made Robeson's films so impressive was Robeson himself. Audiences were always aware of his powerful personal presence, his infectious smile and his engaging, almost mythical personality. These attributes virtually overcame, perhaps even obscured, the specific roles he played, propelling him into yet another of his roles as one of the great African American trailblazers in American cultural and political history.

Chapter 6:

PAUL ROBESON
THE SINGER

OF THE PEOPLE WHO KNOW OF ONLY ONE feature of Paul Robeson's multifaceted life, a large percentage, perhaps most, know of his stature and reputation as a concert and recording star. Even those who know little or nothing about his acting career and his controversial political activism that led to his blacklisting and obliteration from the broader historical record, often recall that he was a major singer. For decades, his concerts and records were extremely well received throughout the world and were striking commercial successes, and made Robeson a wealthy man until his income evaporated during the infamous Red Scare of the 1950s. Those who heard him in person, and those who hear his voice even now, recognize one of the great voices in musical history. In 1935, famed Italian conductor Arturo Toscanini was reported to have said of Robeson's contemporary and friend Marian Anderson that, "a voice like [hers] is heard once in a hundred years." It would not be an exaggeration to apply the same observation to Paul Roberson's bass-baritone voice.

As noted in the chapters on his acting career on stage and in film, his performance of "Ol' Man River," with music by Jerome Kern and lyrics by Oscar Hammerstein II, became his signature song throughout his illustrious singing career. In virtually every concert he performed, and in most of his records, that song made a central appearance. Audiences came to expect it, sometimes demanding an encore performance. But the story about Robeson's change of lyrics in "Ol Man River" reflects his political development and his growing commitment to using his magnificent voice as a public forum for disseminating his progressive social ideology.

Jules Bledsoe first sang Hammerstein's lyrics in 1927 in the original stage production of *Show Boat*, using the original words: "Niggers all work on the Mississippi." In 1928, Robeson himself sang those same words. By the 1930s, however, he changed the word "Niggers" to "Darkies." In contemporary terms, that change seems marginal, even trivial, but at the time it was significant. Moreover, he later changed additional language from, "There's an ol' man called the Mississippi, that's the ol' man that I'd like to be," to, "There's an ol' man called the Mississippi, that's the ol' man I *don't* like to be." He also changed, "You gets a little drunk and you lands in jail," to, "you *show a little grit* and you lands in jail." Finally, in the most significant lyrical change, "I'm tired of livin' and scared of dyin'" became, "I *must keep fightin' until I'm dyin.'*" Hammerstein was reported to be unhappy with Robeson's changes, but overwhelmingly, his audiences and the world generally appreciated the transformation of his signature song from a ballad of lament and resignation to a song of protest and defiance.

Paul Robeson began singing long before performing and transforming "Ol' Man River." His musical talent was obvious even in childhood, particularly in his family home and in his father's church. He shined in the glee club at Somerville High School and later in the home concerts of the Rutgers College glee club. But his professional efforts as a singer began in earnest after he met Larry Brown in England in 1922. Brown had already achieved a strong reputation as the accompanist for Roland Hayes and as a talented arranger of black spirituals. Back in New York, they decided to work together, a professional partnership and friendship that lasted for thirty-five years during Robeson's singing career. The men worked extremely well together and Larry Brown was a powerful influence in Robe-

Larry Brown

son's discovery and commitment to black spirituals and folk music, and to the folk music of other groups of people, especially those resisting oppression like his fellow African Americans. Brown and Robeson traveled the world for his concerts, and Brown played the piano and occasionally joined Robeson in various duets.

> **A full account of Paul Robeson's life and career as a singer could justify an entire book.**

And some highlights of his concert and recording work are vital to an understanding of his interrelated artistic roles in drama, film and music. Eslanda Robeson, his tireless manager, saw that he could have a successfully parallel career as a concert artist and that black spirituals, as Robeson could majestically interpret them, would be one of the central foundations for his success.

Although he had performed in a formal concert in Boston in 1924, as well as in a few private settings, Robeson's first major concert appearance was in New York on April 19, 1925, which set the tone for many of his subsequent concerts and recordings. An overflow audience (with many more turned away) heard him sing Negro spirituals exclusively, with accompanist Larry Brown, including "Go Down, Moses," "Joshua Fit de Battle of Jericho," "Swing Low, Sweet Chariot," "Balm in Gilead," "Bye 'n' Bye," and several others that became hallmarks of his musical performances until his retirement from artistic and public life. Robeson sang sixteen songs in that concert and an additional sixteen encores, leaving him exhausted but exhilarated with this new dimension to his emerging artistic outlet. This concert catalyzed his reputation as a concert singer, which would endure for the remainder of his life. It also cemented his powerful link to his own African American heritage, an identity that pervaded all features of his subsequent artistic and political activities.

Robeson was among the first major African American concert performers, including Roland Hayes and Marian Anderson, to elevate and popularize spirituals, an achievement of huge musical, historical and political significance. First brought to wide public attention by the Fisk Jubilee Singers from Nashville, Tennessee, in tours in Europe and America in the 1870s, spirituals were powerful expressions of religious faith that also expressed heartfelt messages by an oppressed people.. Some spirituals expressed resistance to slavery and oppression and sometimes served as coded messages to slaves seeking to escape their bondage. Decades later, owing partly to Robeson's influence, these songs were vital to the musical dimension of the modern civil rights movement from the mid 1950s through the early 1970s.

Robeson was not entirely self-taught as a vocalist. In 1926, he studied with vocal coaches Teresa Armitage and Frantz Proschowsky and learned how to preserve his voice in light of the frequency of his performances. He also learned to develop his range and his repertoire as a singer, while continuing to devote some concerts entirely to black spirituals and folk songs. Between drama and film obligations, he and Brown performed numerous concerts throughout Europe and the United States.

His early concert success also led to the release of his recordings, which continued throughout his creative life. These records enabled listeners who could not attend live concerts to hear his magnificent voice. His first releases, four double-sided records in 1925, contained his classics like "Joshua Fit de Battle of Jericho" and "Bye 'N Bye." They sold extremely well, bringing Robeson substantial additional income. Other record-ings included traditional American southern tunes like "Dear Old Southland," "Sleepy Time Down South," "Carry Me Back to Green Pastures," "Old Folks at Home," and other similar songs. These early efforts were different from the more socially conscious works of his later concert and recording career.

From the late 1920s onward, Robeson added an educational dimension to his concert performances. He offered comments between his songs, providing his interpretations of the spir-ituals and of the other songs he began singing in his per-formances. These comments were thoughtful and informative, reflecting his serious research and depth of musical knowledge. He also incorporated parts from his theatrical performances into his concerts, especially the last scene from *Othello*, where he slays Desdemona. Regularly, he prefaced his excerpt by noting that Shakespeare's tragic Moor came from, "an Africa of equal stature."

As Robeson deepened his personal knowledge and his po-litical consciousness, he expanded his musical repertoire, including the music of other people, especially those from oppressed groups and cultures throughout the world. Many of his concert efforts also reflected his passion to learn new languages, including various African languages; in England, he had enrolled in the School of Oriental Studies at the Uni-versity of London, and augmented his studies by studying and listening to the folk songs of many cultures.

Folk music had become a chief focus of his musical performances on stage and in his recordings.

By the mid 1930s, Robeson's concerts also included tradi-tional British folk songs like "Oh No, John," which he con-tinued performing throughout his singing career. He added songs from many other lands throughout the 1930s, from Russia, Ireland, Wales and elsewhere. His concerts regularly contained songs where he sang the lyrics in their original languages and in English, switching seamlessly between them. One of his favorites was "The Song of the Volga Boat-men," where Robeson switched imperceptibly from English to Russian during the performances. Some critics, trying to limit him to his African American roots, seemed somewhat disconcerted with his expanded range, but audiences continued to flock to his concerts.

As his political views became more radical, his concert and recording repertory began to include topical and protest songs dealing with themes that reflected his social ideology. These became staples of his performance for the remainder of his career. Among others, these included "Kevin Barry," which told the story of the martyred Irish republican soldier whom the British executed in 1920 for his participation in an IRA operation that resulted in the deaths of three British soldiers; "Joe Hill," which celebrated the life, and mourned the death, of the Swedish-American Industrial Workers of the World labor agitator and songwriter Joe Hill, who was executed by firing squad in Utah for a murder that many scholars believe he did not commit;

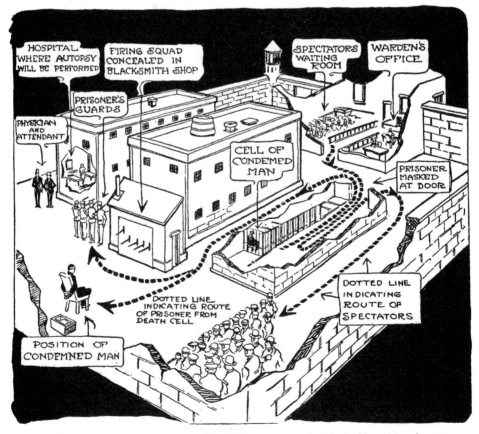

Diagram of the execution of Joe Hill, first published in the Cleveland Press, November 1915

"The Four Insurgent Generals," ("Los Quatro Generales") which attacked the four fascist generals, including Francisco Franco who started the Spanish Civil War by mounting a successful insurgency in 1936 against the Loyalist government in Spain—Robeson sang in both English and Spanish; and "The Peat Bog Soldiers," ("Die Moorsoldaten"), sang by Robeson in both English and German, which communist and socialist prisoners in a Nazi concentration camp in Bogermor wrote in 1933, and which later became a Loyalist anthem during the Spanish Civil War.

Although Robeson admired jazz musicians like Dizzy Gillespie, Ella Fitzgerald, Duke Ellington, Thelonious Monk and others, this was not part of his musical repertory. Neither did he sing the blues, except for a recording of "The St. Louis Blues" in 1934. He had a longer record with classical selections throughout his singing career. Some examples of his classical efforts included Bedrich Smetana's "Freedom," which he sang in English and Czech; Felix Mendelssohn's "Lord God of Abraham"; Wolfgang Amadeus Mozart's "O' Isis and Osiris" from "The Magic Flute"; several selections from Modest Mussorgorsky and Antonin Dvorak and a stirring rendition of Beethoven's "Ode to Joy" from the *Ninth Symphony*, with words by Friedrich Schiller, known as the "Song of Peace," which he sang in English and German. (All of these selections, and many others, are available to contemporary listeners in CD form and on YouTube through a simple Internet search.)

In 1939, Paul Robeson made musical and broadcast history when he recorded his "Ballad for Americans," written by John Latouch and Earl Robinson for a Works Projects Administration theater project. Originally entitled "The Ballad for Uncle Sam," it was changed when Norman Corwin, the producer of the popular radio program "Pursuit of Happiness Hour," booked Robeson, who had recently returned to the United States after successful concerts in Europe to sing the song for a national radio audience. On November 5, 1939, six hundred people were in the studio audience when the CBS chorus and orchestra backed Robeson as he sang this song in praise of ordinary Americans making the country strong and great. The audience went wild with enthusiasm and the song became a huge national hit. Victor Records recorded

"Ballad for Americans" and the Republican Party opened its 1940 convention with a chorus that sang the patriotic ballad.

The song itself reflected the ideology of the "Popular Front," when American radicals and Communists made patriotism and Americanism a central feature of their cultural expressions. The lyrics highlighted an early multiculturalism and a powerful sense of national unity, especially in light of the impending threat from fascisms in Europe. An example from the song can be seen in the following lyrics:

> I'm just an Irish, Negro, Jewish, Italian, French and English, Spanish, Russian, Chinese, Polish, Scotch, Hungarian, Litwak, Swedish, Finnish, Canadian, Greek and Turk and Czech and double-check American—I was baptized Baptist, Methodist, Congregationalist, Lutheran, Atheist, Roman Catholic, Orthodox, Jewish, Presbyterian, Seventh-Day Adventist, Mormon, Quaker, Christian Scientist—and lots more.

The song ended with a dramatic appeal for an inclusive national vision:

> Simple as a hit tune, deep as our valleys
> High as our mountains, strong as the people who made it,
> For I have always believed it,
> And I believe it now,
> And you know who I am,
> America!

To many contemporary listeners, some of these lyrics may sound overly romanticized and sentimental. At the time, in a nation emerging from the Great Depression, Robeson's voice promoted some much needed optimism while cementing his reputation as one of the most accomplished and beloved singers of his era. He repeated his performance of "Ballad for Americans" in several live concerts, most notably in Chicago before a huge crowd in Grant Park and in the largest crowd ever at the time at the Hollywood Bowl in Los Angeles.

The Hollywood Bowl amphitheater by Matthew Field October 1, 2005

Throughout his long concert career, Robeson performed in scores of venues in the United States, Canada, the Caribbean and Central America, Europe (including the Soviet Union) and Australia. As he became more politically engaged, several individual concerts stood out as milestones in his successful quest to unite his creative efforts with his political convictions. Some of these were formal concert performances while others were more informal settings and unusual arrangements; regardless of the venue, Robeson used his voice to express his views about contemporary issues, and to defy the restrictions that the US government had placed upon him.

The Spanish Civil War from 1936 to 1939 was a watershed turning point in Robeson's political radicalization (more in depth in Chapter Seven). In January 1938, Robeson and his wife decided to visit war-torn Spain to express their support for the republic against Franco's fascist onslaught, supported by Adolf Hitler's Nazi regime in Germany. During their time in Spain, the Robesons met with loyalist soldiers, mostly with those fighting with the International Brigades, which were volunteer troops from over fifty nations, including representatives of the US from the Abraham Lincoln Brigade, which included communists, socialists and nonsectarian leftists, among others fighting against fascism. Robeson was deeply moved in his meetings with these soldier-volunteers, many of who had heard his songs and had seen his films. He sang several times for them at locales near the battlefront, having responded to their requests and made one memorable performance in Madrid when he was recognized in the audience at a Cervantes performance. His songs were familiar, and included "Ol' Man River," "Joshua," "Water Boy," and others, as well as numbers from some of his recent motion pictures. These informal performances were huge morale boosters for loyalist soldiers and supporters. After his return from Spain, he continued to sing at fundraisers and other events on behalf of the beleaguered Spanish Republic in England, Scotland, Wales and France.

Despite Paul Robeson's long and controversial support of the Soviet Union, which caused him enormous suffering in the United States, he gave one performance in Moscow in 1949 that reflected some ambivalence for Soviet policy, and affirmed his strong identification with Jews and Jewish culture. In June 1949, Robeson arrived for one of his frequent visits to the Soviet Union and became uneasy at signs of growing Soviet anti-Semitism, including persecution, arrests and even murders of prominent Jewish figures, including Robeson's personal friends, by Stalin's secret police. At a major concert in Moscow, broadcast to 180 million Soviet people, Robeson sang many of his usual songs, including black spirituals, "Joe Hill," "Ol' Man River," and others in several languages.

After thunderous applause and demands for an encore, Robeson told the audience in Russian that he would sing the song of the Jewish resistance fighters in the Warsaw Ghetto, "Zog Nit Keynmol," which he performed in Yiddish. He translated the song's words into Russian before singing:

Never say that you have reached the very end,

When leaden skies a bitter future may portend, For

sure the hour for which we yearn will yet arrive,

And our marching steps will thunder: we survive!

Robeson sang passionately and the audience, including

many Jewish members, responded in kind. But Soviet censors removed his remarks to the audience before he sang and the Western press said nothing about the concert or its dramatic ending. It nevertheless marked a level of complexity and ambiguity in Robeson's otherwise uncritical support of Stalin and the Soviet Union.

The year 1949 marked another dramatic Robeson concert in a highly charged political context, albeit with a profoundly different setting from that of Moscow's Tchaikovsky Concert Hall.

After his return to the United States, Robeson found himself the subject of growing political controversy as the Cold War intensified.

In mid-August 1949, People's Artists, a New York radical theatrical agency, announced that Robeson would give his fourth annual benefit concert for the Harlem Chapter of the Civil Rights Congress outside Peekskill, New York on August 27. The previous three concerts had been successful and had gone on without incident. This time, however, the local media ran hostile stories about Robeson, declaring his presence unwelcome. Local groups like the Chamber of Commerce and the Joint Veterans Council added to the hostility by calling for an anti-Robeson demonstration because of his left-wing beliefs and activism.

When Robeson and Larry Brown arrived in Peekskill, they found that a group of angry anti-Communists from the American Legion, the Veterans of Foreign Wars and other conservative groups had organized a massive demonstration against the concert. The anti-Robeson mob shouted anti-Semitic and anti-black language like "kike" and "nigger," as well as other invective, forcing the cancellation of the performance. The mob threw rocks and later attacked the concert attendees, putting several Robeson supporters in the hospital. The police stood around and did nothing to prevent the violence.

Protesting the violence, Robeson announced a rescheduled concert in Peekskill for September 4, 1949. Once again, protest mobs convened to try to prevent a Robeson concert. More anti-black and anti-Semitic remarks were hurled at the concert visitors, and death threats were commonplace. Robeson was hung in effigy in Peekskill in an especially vile display of hatred. This time, however, thousands of union guards, many World War II veterans, were there to protect Robeson, Brown and the other performers. Pete Seeger was an early performer and Robeson, ringed with bodyguards, followed with ten songs, including "Let My People Go" and concluding with "Ol' Man River," with its altered lyrics that included, "I must keep fightin' until I'm dyin." Robeson was transported home safely, but again the crowd was attacked

brutally; cars and busses were over-turned and windows smashed, and more than one hundred people were injured. Again, the police did nothing and New York Governor Thomas Dewey later claimed that communist forces and agitators had provoked the riot. It was a prelude to the civil rights movement a decade later, when police and southern politicians would likewise defend lawless actions against nonviolent African American and other advocates for racial equality.

Thomas E. Dewey

Despite the violence, Robeson's Peekskill concert served as an inoculation against the growing internal threat of fascism in America. Pete Seeger, one of the performers at the

September 4 concert, maintains persuasively that the collective re-sistance among the concert goers and supporters throughout the country was a key factor in pre-venting demagogues, especially FBI Director J. Edgar Hoover, from im-plementing plans to suspend habeas corpus and imprison some twelve thousand Americans sus-pected of disloyalty, including peo-ple like Seeger and Robeson. Seeger analogizes the resistance at Peek-skill to the vaccination against

Pete Seeger, half-length portrait, singing while playing banjo, 1955. Palumbo, Fred, photographer.

smallpox; in this incident, enough people saw a sufficient glimpse of domestic fascism to prevent its larger, more dangerous eruption.

Throughout most of the 1950s, Paul Robeson had his passport revoked because of his left-wing political views and actions, preventing him from traveling abroad. Astonishingly, this ban extended to Canada, which did not require a passport for entry into the country by US citizens. The Canadian Mine, Mill and Smelter Workers had invited him for a concert in Vancouver, but the US Immigration and Naturalization Service, working in conjunction with Canadian authorities, denied his entry on January 31, 1952. Crossing into Canada would have subjected him to a five-year prison term and a $10,000 fine. Defying the spirit but not the letter of the ban on his travel, Robeson presented two concerts at the Canadian border in 1952 and 1953 in Blaine, Washington, on a flatbed truck a foot from the international boundary.

On May 18, 1952, Robeson sang to approximately forty thousand people, thirty-five thousand of who amassed on the Canadian side. Robeson's concert consisted of his traditional spirituals and political songs. In August 1953, he reprised the Peace Arch concert, this time ending with a long and eloquent speech detailing his political views and reaffirming his resistance to the travel ban and the blacklist he faced in the United States. The speech was eloquent and passionate, and it was all the more remarkable given the stress that Robeson and his family faced amidst governmental persecution and economic oppression. His songs were similar to what he sang the year before, and he added the Chinese marching song "Chin Chin," celebrating the recent communist victory in China.

In a different but equally dramatic concert in 1957, Robeson gave a transatlantic performance by telephone transmission to a large group of Welch miners and supporters; they had sponsored an Eisteddfod, a traditional festival that dated back to the seventh century. (He had given such a concert by phone to an audience in England earlier that year.) Robeson felt deeply moved by the Welsh invitation to appear in person and expressed these feeling in his opening remarks to the audience following Union President William

Portrait of Harry Belafonte, singing, 1954 Feb. 18

Paynter's greetings. Following his songs, consisting mainly of his usual selections, the Treorchy Male Voice Chorus sang for Robeson, adding a huge emotional element to this highly unusual concert. The concert was broadcasted from his brother Ben's church and was financed and organized by Harry Belafonte. In 1958, after he obtained his passport following a protracted battle, Robeson honored his pledge to appear in Wales at the autumn Eisteddfod to thank the miners for their unwavering support.

In 1958, Robeson began a triumphant if somewhat brief return to active public artistic life. After an eleven-year absence, he took the stage again at Carnegie Hall in New York City on May 9, a month after his sixtieth birthday. Unlike the Peekskill experience, there were no riots or demonstrations protesting his concert appearance. Accompanied by Alan Booth, another talented African American musician who shared Robeson's social vision (and his accompanist in the Welsh transatlantic concert), Robeson sang in English, German, Russian, Chinese, Hebrew and Yiddish. His enthusiastic audience also heard his *Othello* excerpt and some general repartee with the crowd. When he sang "Jacob's Ladder," he made a subtle change in the lyrics from, "we're soldiers of the cross," to, "we're soldiers in this fight." Midway through this selection, he asked the audience to join in, which they did enthusiastically. The concert was recorded by Vanguard and it remains available to this day.

Two weeks later Robeson repeated the Carnegie Hall performance to another sold-out audience. This would be his final appearance in that venerable forum; his debut occurred in 1929. Both 1958 concerts drew strongly positive reviews and it was clear that Paul Robeson had returned as a premier concert singer.

During his long years of internal exile, Robeson managed to sing in private left-wing settings and in black churches, including the AME Zion church in Harlem where his brother Ben served as pastor. He made recordings under his own label, Othello Recording Company, which his son Paul, Jr. ran from 1953 to 1955. This allowed Robeson an artistic outlet when commercial opportunities were closed to him because of the blacklist. It was also a time of severe physical and mental debilitation, exacerbated by the turmoil of governmental persecution and politically inspired economic boycotts against him.

Musically, Paul Robeson's influence was both wide and continuing. Probably his most sustained impact was on the emerging folk music culture from the 1940s through the 1960s, which has continued in somewhat diminished form ever since. Some of Robeson's folk singing contemporaries like Woody Guthrie, Pete Seeger, Joe Glazer, Oscar Brand, Josh White, the Almanac Singers and, slightly later, the Weavers (with singers Seeger, Lee Hays, Ronnie Gilbert and Fred Hellerman), all traveled in the same left-wing circles as Robeson, singing topical songs, although their voices and singing styles were vastly different. In 1949, People's Artists, closely associated with the Communist Party, organized folk concerts and Robeson was involved with its efforts. It also published a folk song magazine called *Sing Out!* and Robeson appeared with others on the cover of the July 1951 issue.

Robeson had a direct influence on some prominent American folksingers. Foremost among them has been Harry Belafonte, who had heard Robeson sing black spirituals and Welsh and Russian folk songs. Those experiences led Belafonte to see the power of folk music as a tool for social criticism and change and informed his personal commitment to combine his passion for politics and art. Historian Robbie Lieberman reports in *My Song Is My Weapon* that folksinger and musicologist Jerry Silverman had his first contact with "people's music" when he heard Robeson sing at a rally supporting the Spanish Republic. Lieberman's father Ernie Lieberman was also a prominent younger political folksinger whose musical beginnings emerged from the early 1950s.

Odetta (Odetta Holmes), sometimes known as "the voice of the civil rights movement," had performed on the same bill with Robeson in the early 1950s and was clearly influenced by his political vision in his singing. As a teenager, Mary Travers of the socially oriented folk group Peter, Paul and Mary, had been interested in the voice and political songs of Paul Robeson. From the 1960s to the present, such performers as Phil Ochs, Tom Paxton, Bob Dylan, Joan Baez, Judy Collins, Holly Near, Tracy Chapman, Ani DiFranco

Odetta at the Burg Waldeck-Festival 1968, Germany. *Mirdsson, Sverrir, photographer.*

and Bruce Springsteen have all kept Robeson's political folk singing tradition alive, regardless of how knowledgeable of his efforts they may or may not have been. Folksinger Billy Bragg likewise continues the tradition of radical social and political commentary in the United Kingdom. Bass-baritone Sir Willard White from Jamaica was also inspired as a child by Robeson and later recorded, "The Paul Robeson Legacy," with his rendition of his spirituals and other ballads.

In recent years, several major contemporary stage actors and singers have performed one-person presentations about the life and times of Paul Robeson. Avery Brooks, for example, has played Robeson in Philip Hays Dean's *Paul Robeson*, where Brooks sings several of Robeson's classic songs admirably throughout the performance. Stogie Kenyatta, Tayo Aluko and KB Solomon have all performed their personal interpretations of Robeson and his life of triumphs and travails, with powerful musical interludes. Solomon in particular brings a rich bass-baritone voice and personal manner that closely resembles those of Robeson as he emulates the master's rendition of various classics.

Robeson's musical legacy is powerful and enduring. The revival of his reputation and his historical restoration generally have promoted and deepened scholarly and public understanding of his comprehensive musical contributions. This remains an incomplete and continuing process. The widespread availability of his singing through recordings and the Internet ensures that more audiences will be exposed to his extraordinary voice and the astonishing range of his songs during his forty-plus years as a concert and recording star. Those audiences exist and continue to grow in the United States and throughout the world.

Chapter 7:

PAUL ROBESON
THE INTERNATIONAL
POLITICAL ACTIVIST

PAUL ROBESON'S COMMITMENTS TO POLITICAL ACTIVISM, both internationally and domestically, were among his most significant contributions to his native land. His political activities were numerous and diverse, encompassing speeches and organizing efforts that addressed the major international and domestic events and issues of the twentieth century. The origins of this activism can be traced back to his numerous encounters with racism from his early childhood, through his student days at Rutgers College, to his truncated legal career and into his multiple efforts as a performing artist. But he developed his mature political identity some decades later and this political focus occupied much of his attention for the greater part of his adult life.

Like the focus of this book as a whole, the complexity and breadth of Robeson's political involvement is best explored thematically rather than chronologically. The division of his political activism into international and domestic dimensions develops an introductory understanding of this powerful feature of his life, and deserves deeper exploration in the more detailed sources presented in the Bibliography. The thematic focus likewise locates Robeson's politics in the broader context of his artistic life, especially since his efforts as a stage actor and most notably as a singer sought to integrate his social and political vision as thoroughly as possible. Robeson expressed some of his international political concerns, of course, in America just as he expressed some of his domestic political concerns during his times abroad.

Robeson's political work was highly controversial, especially his long identification with the Soviet Union and his obvious sympathy with the United States Communist Party. Although his admiration for foreign and domestic communism was pronounced (and at times uncritical), it was far from the exclusive focus of his political identity and it was itself nuanced and complex. He was not a member of the Communist Party and his defense of the Soviet Union stemmed, at least in part, from his opposition to fascism and racism. His politics became the most well known feature of his public identity to millions of people throughout the world, and eventually generated catastrophic consequences for his economic station, his physical and psychological health and his legacy.

As a young man, Paul Robeson was always conscious of his outsider status as a black person in a white-majority society. His father impressed upon him the dignity of his people and the need to promote pride for their accomplishments. His own actions implemented that ideal, especially through his academic, athletic and artistic excellence. He was not a political activist as a college and law student, although he was conscious of the political developments in society during those periods. For a long time, he held the view that his own artistic development and reputation would be the best strategy against injustice, especially against the endemic racism in America.

Paul Robeson began his long political journey when he was in England. It was here that he first explored African culture and its close linkages both to his personal racial identity and to the subsequent struggle against European colonialism in Africa. Early in 1933, he and Eslanda enrolled in London University jointly to learn about African language and culture.

Paul began by studying Swahili, Yoruba, Efik, Twi and several other African languages, fully understanding the inextricable connections between language and culture.

The next year, he wrote a statement in a book of articles entitled *What I Want From Life*, which pervaded his political consciousness for the remainder of his life: "[I]n my music, my plays, my films, I want to carry this central idea: to be African. Multitudes of men have died for less worthy ideals; it is even more eminently worth living for."

This vision enabled him to ground his growing sense of internationalism securely in his African roots. Like many black artists, intellectuals and political figures, this African consciousness enabled him to find a strong foundation for overcoming the sense of inferiority that millions of black people felt about themselves in societies that devalued their contributions, and often dehumanized them. Robeson began to feel that Western societies had promoted a caricature of Africa as a continent of barbaric tribes, devoid of genuine civilization and achievement—a view that permeated the dominant entertainment and art in Europe and the United States. This inevitably led to the obliteration of a more authentic view of African history and culture.

> **Above all, Robeson's focus on African culture gave him the history that Western society had stolen, and he realized that a people without a history is doomed to political impotence.**

During his time in England, Robeson had made contact with several Africans, including Nnamdi Azikiwe, Jomo Kenyatta and Kwame Nkrumah, who subsequently became anti-colonial liberation figures and future leaders of their independent African nations. He also met C. L. R. James, the radical Caribbean social and political theorist and starred in his play *Toussaint L'Ouverture* in London. These associations likely reinforced Robeson's growing sense of black identity with its powerful African roots. But his belief that Africans possessed some special essence, some deeper reservoir of emotion and intuition, never led him to the kind of separatist ideology represented by Marcus Garvey and his followers. He also never embraced a narrow black nationalism that excluded or impeded his passionate commitment to international unity and to the interests of oppressed people all over the world.

Portrait photograph of Kwame Nkrumah. Source: Africa Through a Lens. Currently held by The National Archives (United Kingdom).

Robeson attempted to infuse his artistic work with his growing African consciousness. As Chapter Four reveals, he sought to imbue the character of Othello with a strong racial presence and he regularly spoke and wrote about that character as an African. His films were far less successful in promoting a dignified African vision, leading him to abandon that feature of his artistic career. As a singer, he performed black spirituals and selections in various African languages as an affirmation of his racial status and heritage. In remarks during his concerts, he regularly paid homage to African musical creativity.

Robeson's political focus on Africa also had a huge organizational component, directed primarily against Western colonial domination of the African continent. In London in 1937, he contributed funds toward the New York-based International Committee on African American Affairs (ICAA), headed by Max Yergan, whom Robeson had met in England, and who would later play a major role in Robeson's political life. When he and Robeson met, Yergan was an engaging black American intellectual with a pronounced communist identification. (Later in his life, he turned into a tragic caricature of himself, becoming a rabid anti-communist who near the end of his life became an apologist for the racist apartheid system in South Africa.)

In 1941, the ICAA became the Council on African Affairs (CAA). Back in the US, Paul Robeson became the chairman of the organization, which linked the struggles of African Americans and those of the colonized peoples in Africa, Asia and elsewhere. It promoted independence movements in India and throughout Africa. It supported the efforts of the African National Congress in South Africa and was an early opponent of the repressive and racist apartheid government there.

Early in its existence, the CAA attracted support from many liberals, including Franz Boas, E. Franklin Frazier, Mary McLeod Bethune, Adam Clayton Powell and Ralph J. Bunche. Radical participants with ties or sympathies to the Communist Party included Robeson, Yergan, W .E. B. Du Bois and Alphaeus Hunton. In its anti-colonial struggle, the CAA encountered a dramatic setback in 1945 at the United Nations. Robeson and his colleagues had hoped that the United States and its western allies, flush with victory over the Axis powers,

Poster from Office of War Information. Domestic Operations Branch. News Bureau, 1943.
Charles Henry Alston, 1907-1977, Artist

would sympathize with the emerging liberation movements throughout the world. The CAA, then the most important American organization concerned with Africa, wanted strong US support for third world independence under UN trusteeship.

The United States, however, to the extreme dismay of Robeson and the CAA, introduced proposals that provided no limits on Western colonial occupation, and inhibited actions that would lead towards self-government. Robeson expressed his discontent both to President Truman and to the Chair of the US delegation to the United Nations to no avail. He and his CAA colleagues became increasingly disenchanted with world developments in the immediate postwar era. By the early 1950s, the CAA was ensnared in the anti-communist fervor of the early Cold War era in America. Many of its liberal supporters abandoned the organization, and its radical leaders, including Robeson and Du Bois, were under increasing attack as subversives. In 1955, the Council on African Affairs disbanded, bowing under the weight of severe government repression and financial hardship. Advocacy for African liberation was tainted as a "communist" cause and the US government increasingly supported the interests of Western colonial powers throughout the developing world.

Also in 1955, Robeson sent a robust support message to the Asian-African Conference in Bandung, Indonesia. This Conference was organized to promote Asian and African economic, cultural and political cooperation, and to oppose colonialism from the major world powers. Robeson's statement reiterated his well-known anti-imperialist views and reaffirmed his identification with peoples of color in third world nations.

As early as 1948, he made an appearance in London to protest the new apartheid policy that South African National Party Prime Minister D. F. Malan and his extreme racist colleagues created in the Union of South Africa. In 1954, Robeson sent a statement to African National Congress leader Oliver Tambo expressing his solidarity

> One feature of Paul Robeson's African political advocacy that emphasizes his role as powerful forerunner in so many dimensions of human achievement remains largely unknown to his day: he was one of the first public figures to call dramatic public attention to the vicious apartheid regime in South Africa, long before the issue became a major world concern.

with the South African liberation struggle. In his 1958 book *Here I Stand,* he made the point clearly: "Can we oppose White Supremacy in South Carolina and not oppose the same vicious system in South Africa?"

The rest of the world woke up to the South African struggle following the Sharpeville massacre in 1960, the imprisonment of Nelson Mandela, the Soweto student uprising of 1976, and the successful world campaign for economic sanctions and divestment that led to the dismantling of apartheid in 1994. Paul Robeson's early moral and political leadership in this struggle set the tone for the later successful actions that catalyzed a peaceful revolution few observers had predicted. The new democratic South Africa owes its existence to men and women of foresight and courage; Robeson is foremost among them.

The Nazi Germany-supported rebellion of fascist generals

> Robeson's African consciousness was the earliest manifestation of his durable political activism, but it took the Spanish Civil War from 1936 to 1939 to mobilize him into a truly public political figure.

against the lawfully elected Republican government of Spain galvanized thousands of intellectuals, artists and laypersons throughout the world. The Spanish Civil War was part of the specter of fascism spreading across Europe, mobilizing extensive outrage and opposition. During that time, the cause of saving the Spanish Republic from fascist rule became Robeson's primary political focus, a cause championed by other luminaries such as Spanish exiles Pablo Casals, Joan Miro, Pablo Picasso and foreigners like Andre Malraux, Ernest Hemingway, George Orwell and David Alfaro Siqueiros, as well as hundreds of others.

Robeson made numerous speaking and singing appearances in support of the republic, including his 1938 appearance on the battlefront as detailed in the previous chapter. He applauded the Soviet Union's support for the Spanish Loyalists and was deeply impressed with communists who had vigorously opposed Franco's fascist rebellion, including the high numbers of communist soldiers serving in the International Brigades. He felt a particularly special kinship with the African American volunteers in the American contingent, the Abraham Lincoln Brigade.

On June 24, 1937, Robeson made a historic appearance at London's Royal Albert Hall on behalf of the beleaguered Spanish Republic. The rally collected substantial funds and Robeson's songs and remarks were broadcast to worldwide audiences of millions. In his remarks, he offered comments that would characterize the remainder of his political life and that would define his essence as an artist and as a human being:

The challenge must be taken up. Fascism fights to destroy the culture which society has created; created through pain and suffering, through desperate toil, but with unconquerable will and lofty vision . . . The artist must elect to fight for freedom or slavery. I have made my choice. I had no alternative . . . I stand with you in unalterable support of the Government of Spain, duly and regularly chosen by its lawful sons and daughters.

85

Robeson's commitment to the anti-fascist struggle in Spain ultimately brought him back to the United States and cemented his identification with progressive political coalitions, including his longtime domestic and international communist associations. Like many others of his generation, the Spanish struggle was the catalyst for his entire personal identification, including his zealous desire to merge his political beliefs with his artistic pursuits.

Another key element of Robeson's political identity and activism was his strong, never ending support of the Soviet Union. Robeson genuinely believed and regularly expressed the view that capitalism promoted the most predatory features of human existence. He believed that capitalism fostered and exacerbated inequality, poverty, racism and economic and social misery for millions of human beings. His moral vision about the superiority of a socialist trans- formation of society reflected the deepest humanistic features of Marxism. And like many intellectuals of his time, he saw the full embodiment of that vision in the success and con- tinued survival of the Soviet Union.

Robeson arrived at this conclusion as a result of his early travels to the Soviet Union. He and his wife first visited in 1934 via train that went through Berlin in Nazi Germany. Robeson's brief German layover proved traumatic and set the stage for the dramatic contrast between his reception and treatment in the Soviet Union. After disembarking from the train in Berlin, Robeson's black skin evoked hostile attention from citizens and Nazi storm troopers. He witnessed firsthand the malignant racism of Nazism that would soon murder millions of innocent human beings. He likened his experience to American lynchings against black people, reinforcing the anti-fascism that pervaded his entire political consciousness.

His arrival in the Soviet Union was markedly different. Robeson's fluent Russian helped to underscore the mutual admiration of the first visit. The Robesons were greeted warmly on the street and thoroughly enjoyed their meetings with cultural luminaries, especially filmmaker Sergei Eisenstein. Robeson was especially impressed with the Soviet treatment of minority groups from the Central Asian regions of the nation—people who had earlier been regarded as "primitives" but who had been accorded full equality under the Soviet Constitution. Upon his return to England, Robeson told the press that he felt like a human being for the first time in the Soviet Union with a sense of full human dignity.

The contrast between Nazi Germany and the Soviet Union allowed Robeson to form a highly favorable view of Soviet communism. At the time, Robeson knew nothing of Stalin's forced collectivization programs and the Ukrainian famine. At least initially, Robeson perceived a strong dichotomy of good versus evil, with the Soviet Union as the major bulwark against the specter of fascism and racism encroaching upon the world as a whole. This attitude was common among pro-Soviet intellectuals throughout the world and Robeson's attitudes were far from uncommon, especially in the 1930s and 1940s.

Throughout the 1930s, Paul Robeson applauded the Soviet Union in his speeches and writings for its support of the Spanish Republic, and for its domestic and international advocacy for people of color. Robeson enrolled his son Paul, Jr. in a Soviet school where he learned the Russian language, history and culture. Although there is little record of Robeson's response to the Soviet purge trials of the late 1930s, he did give an interview in 1936 to his longtime friend, US communist leader Ben Davis, which appeared in the *Sunday Worker* on May 10, 1936:

Benjamin Davis, Jr. (1903-1964)

"They ought to destroy anybody who seeks to harm that great country."

It would not be the last time that he would offer uncritical observations about the Soviet Union and Stalin.

His pro-Soviet speeches and actions were less controversial in the 1930s and the 1940s. The Soviet Union was an ally in the struggle against the Axis powers and many liberal and leftist artists, intellectuals and politicians in Europe and the United States regularly expressed such favorable Soviet sentiments. The German surrender in May 1945 and the Japanese surrender in August 1945 changed the world dramatically and launched Robeson on the downward personal and professional trajectory from which he never recovered in his lifetime.

On October 18, 1945, Robeson received the well-deserved Spingarn Medal, the thirtieth annual award from the National Association for the Advancement for Colored People. This was the organization's highest honor and represented the apex of his public fame. At the ceremony, with guests including W.E.B. Du Bois, Marian Anderson, and top NAACP officials, Robeson launched into a presentation that glorified the Soviet Union while attacking the foreign policy of the new Truman administration. Not long after the speech, NAACP leaders Walter White and Roy Wilkins began attacking Robeson, dividing him from the African American community.

Robeson, however, was profoundly concerned about the ominous threat of war in the new nuclear age.

Pursuing this theme, he went to Paris in April to attend the Congress of the World Partisans of Peace at a time of growing tensions between the Soviet Union and the Western powers. The Paris Conference was a huge affair, with 1,800 delegates including major world political, intellectual and artistic celebrities. Its focus was clearly leftist and generally opposed to American foreign policy. Robeson sang and made familiar comments about peace and the Soviet Union, noting that, "[w]e shall not make war on anyone. We shall not make war on the Soviet Union."

But the Associated Press misreported Robeson's words as, "[i]t is unthinkable that American Negroes would go to war on behalf of those who have oppressed us for a generation. . . against the Soviet Union. . . ." The response in the United States was slanderous and widespread. Robeson was denounced as an enemy of America and his estrangement with his native land and with the black community widened.

He continued to visit the Soviet Union. Chapter Six details his June 1949 Moscow concert shortly after the Paris speech where he sang a Yiddish version of the Warsaw resistance song "Zog Nit Keynmol." By then, Robeson was clearly aware of Stalin's anti-Semitic purges in the Soviet Union and was distressed that he was unable to find some of his Soviet Jewish friends. After repeated inquiries, Soviet authorities brought his friend, Yiddish poet Itzik Feffer, to his hotel room, where Feffer used mute gestures to indicate that the room was bugged and that he himself was a likely target for extermination—a deadly prophecy that transpired with his execution three years later. Robeson's final song was an oblique public criticism of Stalin's terror, but he never repeated that gesture again.

RETURN TO MOSCOW

SOME THINGS HAVE CHANGED...

IN JUNE 1949 PAUL MADE ANOTHER TRIP TO THE SOVIET UNION. HE WAS CONCERNED ABOUT THE FATE OF HIS MANY SOVIET JEWISH FRIENDS... ONE OF THOSE FRIENDS WAS ITZIK FEFFER

UNKNOWN TO PAUL, HIS FRIEND was sent to PRISON

ON THE MORNING OF PAUL'S CONCERT, FEFFER WAS BROUGHT FROM HIS CELL TO PAUL'S HOTEL ROOM.

THE ROOM WAS BUGGED!

FEARING DEATH, ITZIK HAD TO KEEP HIS IMPRISIONMENT SECRET! BUT, HE FOUND A WAY TO USE HAND GESTURES TO COMMUNICATE...

ITZIK WAS A WELL KNOWN RUSSIAN POET AND DECORATED WAR VETERAN!

TCHAIKOVSKY HALL

FEELING POWERLESS... PAUL WANTED TO MAKE A PUBLIC STATEMENT!

91

Robeson's silence must have concealed his private doubts, even his anguish about what he had witnessed. His basic view was that public criticism of the Soviet Union would only exacerbate tensions between the world's superpowers and would strengthen the most retrograde and bellicose forces in the United States. He most likely believed that any public criticism of Stalin and Soviet policies, especially by a person of his fame and public visibility, would contribute to the anti-communist fervor in the United States. That view, if not ultimately persuasive, was plausible at the time.

In 1952, Robeson accepted one of the Stalin Peace Prizes that the Soviet Union awarded to seven recipients. The Prize carried a gold medal and a cash award of about $25,000. The pro-communist left applauded the award, but other reactions were generally critical. In 1953, Stalin died and Robeson wrote a eulogy that he titled "To You Beloved Comrade," where he praised the Soviet leader and said that, "[h]e leaves tens of millions all over the earth bowed in heart-aching relief," and, "[f]orever will his name be honored and beloved in all lands." In 1956, Nikita Khrushchev revealed the full extent of Stalin's crimes to the Soviet people and to the world. Robeson was surely aware of the new Soviet leader's stunning critique of his predecessor, but however disappointed he must have been, he never publicly offered any comments or personal criticisms of the Soviet system, or of its disgraced former dictator and his horrific crimes against humanity.

In the post-war period, Robeson regularly uttered simplistic pro-Soviet statements and engaged in other questionable political rhetoric. He spoke warmly at a dinner honoring Soviet Foreign Minister Andrei Vyshinsky, the notorious prosecutor in Stalin's purge trials of the 1930s. He crusaded passionately for civil liberties, but notably exempted followers of Leon Trotsky of the US Socialist Workers Party, blaming them for "slanders" about Stalin and his alleged police state. These were not Paul Robeson's finest moments.

It is understandable that a talented artist like Robeson would respond positively to a Soviet society that treated him with dignity and acclaim, in contrast to a racially divided America that too often expressed disrespect and disdain for him and his fellow African Americans.

For Robeson and other pro-Communist intellectuals, it may have been difficult to abandon the vision of the Soviet beacon, even in the face of powerful evidence of the growing gap between socialist ideals and Soviet practices. Whatever his reasons, his flawed and troubling silence about Stalinist oppression should be viewed in the deeper perspective of his monumental accomplishments, his powerful intellectual stature and his courageous and outspoken political vision on every other front, including his extraordinary record of progressive political activism domestically explored in the next chapter.

Africa, Spain and the Soviet Union were Paul Robeson's chief international political causes. During his extended stays in England, he also supported labor unions in the British Isles, especially the Welsh miners with whom he developed a strong, long-term relationship. In 1958, he reiterated his strong identification with the British labor movement in *Here I Stand,* recognizing that this early labor movement support in England must lead him back to America to pursue the same pro working-class political agenda. Robeson's political activities intensified on his return to his country of birth. His political efforts in the United States from 1939 until his retirement from public life established him as one of the greatest radical political activists in US history. They contributed immeasurably to the iconic reputation that only now has begun to reemerge.

Chapter 8:

PAUL ROBESON
THE DOMESTIC
POLITICAL ACTIVIST

WHEN AMERICANS THINK OF CIVIL RIGHTS FIGURES AND leaders, they inevitably recall the major personalities of the 1960s like Dr. Martin Luther King and Rosa Parks. Some with greater historical knowledge identify the key historical figures like Frederick Douglass, Ida B. Wells, Marcus Garvey, W.E.B. Du Bois, A. Philip Randolph, Malcolm X and many others.

Few place Paul Robeson in that category, yet another troubling omission born of his obliteration from national memory.

But Robeson's contribution to civil rights activism in the United States was enormous. His advocacy for his own race was at the heart of his political life when he returned from his long sojourn abroad. His numerous speeches and actions against racism in his native land reflected his lifelong experience with personal discrimination as well as the core feature of his identity as a human being. Just as he declared in 1934 in England that he wanted to be African, he vigorously affirmed his racial pride in the Author's Foreword to *Here I Stand* in 1958: "I am a Negro. I live in Harlem–this city with a city, the Negro metropolis of America. And now as I write of things that are urgent in my mind and heart, I feel the press of all that is around me where I live, at home among my people."

Robeson's powerful view of himself as a member of an oppressed minority group was the foundation for his identification with all oppressed groups, in America and elsewhere in the world. But that wider focus, which took numerous forms, was deeply rooted in the African American struggle against centuries of unspeakable violence and discrimination. As he puts it in

Here I Stand, "What future can America have without the free and unfettered contributions of our sixteen millions?"

One of his earliest civil rights activities occurred during World War II and during his iconic run of *Othello* on Broadway. As a former athlete, it was natural for him to participate in the campaign to break the color line in Major League Baseball. This issue had been of profound concern in the black community. Many sportswriters in the black press attacked the "gentleman's agreement" that kept African American players out of the American and National Leagues. The US Communist Party, along with its newspaper, *The Daily Worker*, also mounted a steady moral and political campaign against segregated baseball, which Robeson would likely have followed.

In 1943, Brooklyn communist councilman Peter Cacchione introduced a desegregation resolution, reflecting the party's drive to add sports to its more comprehensive attack on Jim Crow practices. On December 3, 1943, Robeson led a delegation of eight black publishers to the office of Baseball Commissioner Kennesaw Mountain Landis, to meet with the owners of the sixteen major leaguer teams. He spoke passionately and drew on his own experience with racism in sports, such as when he first tried out for the Rutgers football team. He assured the baseball executives that integration would proceed smoothly and that it was, "the best in the American spirit."

After Robeson's presentation, Commissioner Landis informed the press that no law prevented blacks from entering Major League Baseball. Still, the white owners (who applauded Robeson's speech) were reluctant to boldly challenge the existing arrangement that kept black baseball players, including some of America's finest athletes, from competing in the major leagues. Nevertheless, less than two years after Robeson's plea, the Brooklyn Dodgers signed Jackie Robinson to play for its minor league affiliate in Montreal of the International League. In 1947, the Dodgers brought Robinson up to play for the Brooklyn Dodgers, finally breaking the color line. Protracted political pressure from celebrities like Robeson proved crucial in wearing down the resistance to change. Like all civil rights advances, change emerges from political struggle, not from the moral epiphanies of the powerful and privileged.

Jackie Robinson swinging a bat in Dodgers uniform, 1954.

CRUSADE AGAINST LYNCHING

ONE OF PAUL ROBESON'S KEY CIVIL RIGHTS ACTIVITIES AFTER WORLD WAR II WAS HIS LEADERSHIP IN THE CRUSADE AGAINST LYNCHING, WHICH HAS BEEN THE SCOURGE OF AFRICAN AMERICAN LIFE AND AMERICAN HISTORY SINCE THE END OF THE CIVIL WAR!

ROBESON READ "THE NEW EMANCIPATION PROCLAMATION" AT THE LINCOLN MEMORIAL IN WASHINGTON DC ON SEPTEMBER 23, 1946

NEARLY 3,500 AFRICAN AMERICANS WERE LYNCHED IN THE UNITED STATES BETWEEN 1892 AND 1968 MOST WERE MEN, BUT MANY WERE WOMEN.

One of Paul Robeson's key civil rights activities before his dramatic eclipse from fame and respectability in the late 1940s was his leadership role in the continuing crusade against lynching, which had been the scourge of African American life—and American history—since the end of the Civil War. Thousands of black men and women had been brutally murdered in the South and elsewhere, some burnt and beaten beyond recognition by domestic terrorists groups like the Ku Klux Klan. This topic had been at the top of the American civil rights agenda for many decades, especially since crusading black journalist Ida B. Wells elevated this horror to national attention. Following the Second World War, many returning black veterans were met with lynch mobs, some murdered in unspeakably grisly ways. Robeson spoke passionately about this renewed anti-black violence at a Madison Square Garden rally on September 12, 1946, calling on President Truman to use his authority to speak out against this racist horror and to mobilize the federal government against the new wave of lynching.

He also decided to organize a crusade against lynching, where he drew the support of W.E.B. Du Bois and Albert Einstein, who agreed to co-chair the Crusade Against Lynching. But the effort drew the opposition of black establishment figures who increasingly separated themselves, and segments of the black community, from Robeson. On September 23, 1946, Robeson read a new Emancipation Proclamation from the foot of the Lincoln Memorial in Washington, D. C. to a large integrated audience.

Later that day, he led a multi-racial delegation that met with President Harry Truman in the White House. Robeson and the other speakers had a confrontational session with the President. They argued that lynching was a national emergency that demanded swift and effective federal action. Truman responded that the time was not yet right for action and that political considerations, presumably fierce opposition from southern legislators, would prevent the passage of an anti-lynching bill. Truman was plainly annoyed at the group's persistence and militancy. Robeson in particular took an appropriately aggressive stance.

Harry S. Truman

He told the President that if the federal government refused to defend its black citizens, blacks would have to defend themselves—a statement that would presage the comments of Malcolm X during the early 1960s. Truman was angry when he ended the meeting, but Robeson offered no apology for his content or tone.

PAUL HAD A CONFRONTATIONAL MEETING WITH PRESIDENT TRUMAN... TRUMAN INTERRUPTED ROBESON, SAYING THE TIME WAS NOT RIGHT FOR FEDERAL ACTION AGAINST LYNCHING!

"IF THE FEDERAL GOVERNMENT REFUSED TO DEFEND ITS BLACK CITIZENS AGAINST MURDER, BLACKS WOULD HAVE TO DEFEND THEMSELVES"

ROBESON'S STRONG WORDS ANTICIPATED THE MILITANT STANCE MANY YEARS LATER OF MALCOLM X.

HIS REMARKS TO PRESIDENT TRUMAN WERE SIMILAR TO MALCOLM'S IN HIS 1964 SPEECH, "THE BALLOT OR THE BULLET"

African Americans had regularly been victimized by lynch mobs and by the judicial process in America. Robeson was acutely aware of this long and degrading history, especially the infamous 1931 Scottsboro case, where nine teenage African American males were accused of rape in a case tinted with racism and legal misconduct. A similar miscarriage of justice occurred during The Trenton Six case in 1948, when New Jersey authorities charged, convicted and sentenced six African American men to death for murdering a white shop-keeper. Robeson spoke out against the injustice of this case.

Robeson sought to bring such legal outrages to international attention when he presented a petition entitled "We Charge Genocide" to the United Nations in New York in 1951. The petition claimed the United States was guilty of genocide under the UN Charter through its failure to act against lynching and institutional racism, which included wrongful executions of African Americans in a racist criminal justice system. Several left-wing luminaries like W.E.B. Du Bois, Benjamin Davis, Los Angeles publisher and activist Charlotta Bass and family members of lynching victims signed the petition. The US government used its influence to squelch the petition, preventing the UN Human Rights Commission from discussion the genocide charge.

Robeson also lobbied vigorously for several other civil rights issues, frequently appearing on picket lines in support of such objectives as a Fair Employment Practices Commission (FEPC), the abolition of the poll tax that prevented blacks from voting in the South, and individual business and entertainment establishments that discriminated against black citizens. In *Here I Stand*, moreover, he devoted two entire chapters to the black freedom struggle. "The Time is Now" attacks "gradualism," the flawed notion that blacks should be patient and wait for gradual change in the oppressive circumstances of their lives. It uses a militant tone in demanding immediate implementation of constitutional rights to minority populations. It also links the American black struggle with third world liberation movements in Asia, Africa and Latin America.

In his chapter, "The Power of Negro Action," Robeson promotes a vision of coherent organization and the power of numbers—the very basis of the modern civil rights movement, then in its infancy. He alluded to the historic Montgomery Bus Boycott of 1956 and made a persuasive argument that the civil rights movement, while enthusiastically welcoming support from all people of goodwill, must be led by African Americans themselves. In the 1964 appendix to his book, written during his retirement from public life, Robeson also offered some observations about the civil rights struggle. Among other things, he commented on the brutal murders of the four young girls in Birmingham a few weeks after the

1963 march on Washington and the murders of Medgar Evers and SNCC volunteers James Chaney, Andrew Goodman and Michael Schwerner in Mississippi. This revealed his continuing interest even while he was physically incapable of active personal participation and leadership.

Robeson's acrimonious 1946 meeting with President Harry Truman and his general leftist views led him in 1948 to the formal electoral process with the insurgent Progressive Party. This left-wing alternative to the Democratic Party and its candidate, Henry Wallace, Franklin Roosevelt's former

Henry A. Wallace

Vice President, sought to defuse the Cold War by establishing peaceful relations with the Soviet Union and by pursuing pro-labor, pro-civil rights domestic policies. The Progressive Party attracted communists and non-communist leftists to its ranks. On January 29, 1948, Robeson became the co-chair of the Henry Wallace for President Committee. He spent an enormous amount of time and energy on the Wallace campaign in 1948, making appearances, delivering numerous speeches and singing at Wallace rallies throughout the nation.

In July 1948, the Progressive Party Convention in Philadelphia nominated Wallace and Senator Glen Taylor of Idaho for Vice President. Robeson, sometimes with his longtime musical accompanist Larry Brown, made campaign tours for the Wallace/Taylor ticket. In the South and elsewhere, they were harassed and the party was regularly subjected to redbaiting because of its communist ranks. While campaigning in the South, Robeson stood by his personal ideals by refusing to speak before segregated audiences. The election results were disappointing. Wallace received only slightly more than a million votes nationwide, with no electoral votes. Most black votes supported Truman's reelection, but Robeson continued and even intensified his political activism.

Paul Robeson's most prominent domestic political work involved his efforts against the political persecution of communists during the Cold War era, which had proven to
be a wave of repression, and a threat to civil liberties.

Many of Robeson's problems resulted from his close and sympathetic association with the US Communist Party as well as his pro-Soviet stance. Although never a member, he vigorously supported party members, including some personal friends, who were charged with criminal offenses under the Smith Act. That act, first passed in 1940, allowed the Department of Justice to prosecute persons for conspiracy to violently overthrow the government.

The trial of twelve Communist Party leaders was held in New York City in 1949. Robeson appeared at the Foley Square Courthouse to greet the defendants and express solidarity with them. After a contentious ten-month trial, with an overtly hostile federal Judge Harold Medina presiding, the defendants were found guilty and Medina sentenced most to five years of imprisonment and fines of $10,000 (one defendant, Robert Thompson, received a lighter sentence because of his distinguished World War II record). Medina also sentenced the defense attorneys to jail for contempt of court, reflecting the growing judicial and political hostility against political dissenters in the United States.

Robeson was never personally indicted during that era, but he protested against the prosecutions of the "second tier" communist leaders. He also protested the increasing power of the FBI and its director J. Edgar Hoover, who unleashed the bureau's considerable resources against anyone he regarded as subversive; Robeson himself had been under government surveillance at least since 1941. The FBI also watched and interrogated his friends and family, adding additional intimidation. With the ascendance of Senator Joseph R. McCarthy of Wisconsin, the anticommunist fervor grew even stronger, encouraging a notable increase in racist sentiment throughout the land and fundamentally augmenting the persecutions and blacklists of leftists and liberals in all fields of endeavor, but especially in entertainment and education. The effect on Robeson was devastating. His concerts and performances were canceled throughout the country.

Joseph Raymond McCarthy

> **No single action was more devastating to Robeson's career, however, than the government's withdrawal of his passport in 1950, which he had held since 1922.**

It resulted in thousands of dollars worth of losses to his income, and additional thousands of dollars worth of legal expenses in the case to restore his right to travel. It prevented him from accepting concert invitations throughout the world, and kept him from promoting his political vision outside the United States. The State Department issued this statement in justification for its decision to prevent him from traveling abroad: "This action is taken because the Department considers that Paul Robeson's travel abroad would be contrary to the best interests of the United States." This was an obvious cover for monitoring and squelching radical dissent. Robeson was demanded to sign an affidavit that he was not a communist in a subsequent meeting with US State Department officials. He refused. Many other leftist dignitaries, including W.E.B. Du Bois, artist Rockwell Kent, journalist and community activist Charlotta Bass, writer Howard Fast and philosopher Corliss Lamont, also had their right to travel restricted.

There was minimal protest in the United States against the State Department's action, and it was confined to leftist circles. International protest was more substantial because of Robeson's continuing stellar reputation abroad. In December 1950, Robeson filed suit in federal court demanding the return of his passport, claiming that the State Department's action violated his First Amendment rights of freedom of speech and association and that it prevented him from practicing his profession as a performing artist. The federal district court dismissed Robeson's suit and his lawyers appealed, setting the stage for a protracted legal battle.

> **In internal exile, Robeson intensified his political activism.**

He continued with the Progressive Party, supporting the 1952 candidacy of radical lawyer Vincent Hallinan for president and Charlotta Bass for vice president. Disappointingly, the ticket received fewer than two hundred thousand votes. Robeson also denounced the convictions of Julius and Ethel

Rosenberg for conspiracy to commit espionage for the Soviet Union. He spoke and sang at a rally to protest their death sentences, which were carried out in June 1953. Moreover, he founded and contributed to the monthly newspaper *Freedom*, authoring regular columns on political topics with the assistance of African American writer Lloyd Brown, who later collaborated with him on *Here I Stand*.

Finally, in a related case in 1958, the United States Supreme Court, in a narrow 5-4 decision in *Kent v. Dulles* (357 US 116), overturned the State Department regulations denying passports to communists and others suspected of disloyalty to the government. Writing for the majority, Justice William O. Douglas, the court's leading progressive member, held that the right to travel is part of the liberty protected under the Due Process Clause of the Fifth Amendment. This was the end of a long eight-year struggle for Robeson to regain his passport. He and Eslanda soon booked passage to London where he shortly resumed his dramatic and concert career.

Capt. Justice William O. Douglas

Robeson devoted an entire chapter of *Here I Stand* to this fundamental human and constitutional right. Of the many points he made in the chapter entitled "Our Right to Travel," he linked his passport troubles with the historical struggles of African Americans. He discussed the freedom of movement that escaped slaves, including his father, asserted for themselves in the absence of any freedoms at all. His point was simple and true: the concept of travel is inseparably linked to the concept of freedom. His most powerful historical example in this chapter was the story of Frederick Douglass, who was denounced in the US press when he spoke for abolition of slavery in England. Like Douglass, Robeson also condemned American racism while traveling and residing abroad, for which he paid a much higher price than his distinguished nineteenth century African American counterpart.

THROUGHOUT THE 1950'S PAUL ROBESON, AND HUNDREDS OF OTHER CREATIVE FIGURES WERE SUBJECT TO SEVERE BLACKLISTING AND PERSECUTION THROUGHOUT THE UNITED STATES.

BLACKLIST

PAUL ROBESON
EDWARD G. ROBINSON
CANADA LEE
AARON COPLAND
BURL IVES
LENA HORNE

LENA HORNE HAD BEEN THE FIRST AFRICAN AMERICAN PERFORMER TO SIGN A LONG-TERM CONTRACT WITH A MAJOR HOLLYWOOD STUDIO!

THE FBI TOOK NOTES OUTSIDE OF PAUL'S HOUSE.

PAUL AND HIS FAMILY WERE BEING SPIED ON!

ROBESON'S ALBUM BECAME UNAVAILABLE IN STORES....

ROBESON'S HERE!

NO LONGER AVAILABLE

topic
TOP.32 E.P.

Robeson challenged yet another ominous threat to civil liberties during his protracted blacklisting and effective "nation arrest." This was an era of legislative "investigations"—"witch-hunts" would be an appropriate term in light of the ferocity that US Senators, Congressman and even state legislators attacked the people they subpoenaed to explain their leftist and liberal beliefs and political associations. Frequently, these investigating committees demanded that witnesses admit to membership in the Communist Party and to name others involved in a purported conspiracy to overthrow the government. These were scarcely information gathering activities in preparation for future legislation; rather, they were inquisitions, designed to intimidate people and to cast a pall over political dissent in America.

The most infamous of these committees was the House Un-American Activities Committee (HUAC), which gained national notoriety in 1947 after holding nine days of hearings into alleged communist influences in the Hollywood movie industry. Many, like Robeson, found it difficult or impossible to work, resorting sometimes to pseudonyms to distribute their screenplays. In the early 1950s, Senator Joseph McCarthy chaired the Senate Permanent Subcom-

> This gave rise to the notorious "Hollywood Ten" case, where celebrated screenwriters who declined to testify were later blacklisted and sentenced to prison for contempt of Congress.

mittee on Investigations, which also conducted these anti-communist crusades, relying substantially on paid informants. In 1953, Eslanda Robeson was summoned before McCarthy's committee, where she responded coolly and intelligently to questions from the senator and committee counsel Roy Cohn, ultimately invoking her Fifth Amendment rights. McCarthy declined to pursue a contempt citation, perhaps in deference to Eslanda's gender.

Paul Robeson himself had an earlier experience with a state investigating committee in California in 1946. Called to testify before the Joint Fact-Finding Committee on Un-American Activities in California, he was questioned by state senator Jack B. Tenney, one of the most retrograde political figures in California's history. This hearing occurred before he had become a public pariah, so the exchange was largely a matter of political and philosophical debate. But during the hearing, Robeson noted that the Communist Party was a legal party, like the Republican and Democratic parties. He pointedly declared, "I am not a communist." He also made clear his vigorous anti-fascism and his profound abhorrence to racism and anti-Semitism.

On May 22, 1956 Paul Robeson was given a subpoena to appear before HUAC in Washington, DC. This came at an especially troubling time for him; by mid-May, Robeson had become seriously depressed, spending time at home, often in bed or doing little or nothing at his desk. This condition, which would take a more severe turn a few years later, disconcerted his friends and family. It followed his prostate surgery in 1955 and Eslanda's mastectomy for breast cancer in the same year; both health scares had a severe effect on his mental state. His physicians believed that he was in serious trouble and advised him not to attend the HUAC hearing. The committee granted a two-week postponement and then Robeson appeared with his counsel, Milton Friedman, and his wife and son.

Despite fears that his depressed state would impede his testimony, Robeson responded defiantly and with the fire and vigor characteristic of his finest artistic performances and political activism. Unlike many witnesses, who cowered before their inquisitors, Robeson took them on, boldly responding to his congressional antagonists and calling their very legitimacy into question. His testimony, as much as that of any other person summoned before HUAC, revealed the true and insidious nature of the modern-day inquisition. Excerpts of that testimony reflect the spirit of his defiance:

MR. ARENS [Committee Staff Director]: Are you now a member of the Communist Party?

MR. ROBESON: Oh, please, please, please.

MR. ARENS: Please answer, will you.

MR. ROBESON: What is the Communist Party? What do you mean by that?

MR. ARENS: Are you now a member of the Communist Party?

MR. ROBESON: Would you like to come to the ballot box when I vote and take out the ballot and see?

MR. ARENS: Have you ever been known under the name John Thomas?

MR. ROBESON: . . . .John Thomas! My name is Paul Robeson, and anything I have to say, or stand for, I have said in public all over the world, and that is why I am here today. . .

MR. ARENS: I put it to you as a fact, and ask you to affirm or deny the fact, that your Communist Party name was "John Thomas."

MR. ROBESON: I invoke the Fifth Amendment. This is really ridiculous. . .

Robeson continued by attacking the Democratic Chairman of the Committee, Representative Francis Walter of Pennsylvania, accusing him of racism by authoring the McCarran-Walter Act that severely restricted immigration to those suspected of being "subversives." Robeson responded to a question by asking Congressman Walter if he was "the author of all the bills that are going to keep all kinds of decent people out of the country?" Walter replied, " No, only your kind."

One of Robeson's most spirited exchanges occurred with Republican Representative Gordon Scherer of Michigan, who pressed him on his ties with the Soviet Union:

MR. SCHERER: Why do you not stay in Russia?

MR. ROBESON: Because my father was a slave, and my people died to build this country, and I am going to stay here, and have a part in it just like you. And no fascist-minded people will drive me from it. Is that clear? I am for peace with the Soviet Union, and I am for peace with China, and I am not for peace with the fascist Franco, and I am not for peace with fascist Nazi Germans. I am for peace with decent people.

MR. SCHERER: You are here because you are promoting the communist cause.

MR. ROBESON: I am here because I am opposing the neo-Fascist cause, which I see arising in these committees. You are like the Alien [and] Sedition Act, and Jefferson could be sitting here, and Frederick Douglass could be sitting here, and Eugene Debs could be here.

Following the hearing, the angry committee members voted unanimously to hold Robeson in contempt. Robeson had indeed shown profound contempt for the committee and its witch hunt proceedings; he had invoked his Fifth Amendment rights to refuse to answer questions and the House of Representatives declined to accept HUAC's recommendation to proceed with a contempt prosecution. Robeson's performance was one of his best in years, remarkable in the hysterical atmosphere of the era. His courageous stand before the committee and the positive responses from the progressive and black press boosted his spirits, lifting him from his depression, at least temporarily.

Another key feature of Paul Robeson's domestic political activism involved his close support of the labor movement. He cherished his ties with several unions, especially the most militant organizations that were part of the progressive coalitions he supported throughout his mature years. He preferred the more militant Congress of Industrial Organizations (CIO) to the American Federation of Labor (AF of L) and vigorously sought to promote black participation in the CIO. In remarks that the United Auto Workers published in 1940 during a campaign to organize the Ford Motor Company, he wrote that the best way for blacks to win justice is by working with white workers in integrated, progressive labor unions. He was unambiguous on this point: "It would be unpardonable for Negro workers to fail to join the CIO." Likewise, he became an honorary member of the National Negro Labor Council, which united black workers with other allies in a struggle for greater job opportunities, fair wages and improved working conditions.

Several labor unions reciprocated with their admiration and affection. He was an honorary member of the National Maritime Union, the Fur and Leather Workers Union, the Food and Tobacco Workers Union, the International Longshore and Warehouse Union and the United Public Workers Union, where he supported the mostly black union workers in the US-controlled Panama Canal Zone with concerts in 1947. He regularly spoke, sang and marched on picket lines for workers throughout the country. He also regularly spoke to individual workers at union picket lines and demonstrations. His labor activism and commitments were inextricably linked to his overall vision of a humane social order where working people lived lives of decency and dignity.

Robeson also paid attention to children as part of his larger social vision. For several summers, Robeson was an honored guest at Camp Wo-Chi-Ca (acronym for Workers Children Camp) in New Jersey, not far from his birthplace. It was one of several left-wing summer camps loosely affiliated with the Communist Party, attracting an interracial population that also included Robeson's son Paul, Jr. Several notable, progressive artists visited Camp Wo-Chi-Ca regularly, providing a huge treat for the young campers. These included Pete Seeger, Canada Lee, Rockwell Kent, Woodie Guthrie, Charles White and Elizabeth Catlett. White and Catlett, who also taught art at the camp, became two of the most renowned African American visual artists of the modern era. No guest, however, was more welcome and honored than Paul Robeson, who regularly spoke with the individual youngsters, sang for them, served on the Board of Trustees and even umpired in a camp intramural baseball game.

Even more unrecognized, Robeson's commitment to the most marginalized populations encouraged him to include them in his own concert tours.

In 1941, for example, he became the first major concert artist to perform for an audience of prison inmates at San Quentin. Seven years later, he sang for the leper settlement on Molokai Island in Hawaii, an event that moved him deeply and that also reflected the profound humanism underlying his entire political life and work.

A treatment of Robeson's domestic political perspective must also consider his powerful commitment to African American and Jewish friendship and solidarity, especially in an era where those historic links are frayed and weakening. From his earliest days, Robeson was intrigued and impressed with Jewish history and culture, spending considerable time with his numerous Jewish friends and associates over the years. In his foreword to *Here I Stand*, he makes his sentiments clear on this point: "I do care—and deeply—about the America of the common people whom I have met across the land. . . , the Jewish people with whom I have been especially close. . . ." Many people, especially among political progressives, have articulated a broad vision of unity among all people, especially the oppressed. Paul Robeson did much more: he *lived* that vision.

Chapter 9:

THE FINAL YEARS AND HIS LASTING LEGACY

WHEN PAUL ROBESON REGAINED
his US passport in 1958, he infused
travel and politics into the final few years
of his active public life. On July 10, 1958, he
and Eslanda boarded a BOAC flight to London,
where they were met with an enthusiastic crowd of friends
and supporters. The general British reception was equally

enthusiastic because he had retained his popularity abroad even while experiencing hostility in America during the 1950s. He resumed his concert performances, teaming up again with longtime accompanist Larry Brown to extremely appreciative audiences and strong reviews. For a brief time, Robeson had returned to a familiar glory.

After a month in London, the Robesons returned to the Soviet Union, to an even more passionate welcome. Singing again, he reprised his traditional songs and added some patriotic Russian selections. During his return trip, he also visited and dined with Premier Nikita Khrushchev. Photographs of the encounter were subsequently used in US news accounts to heighten American hostility toward Robeson for his communist sympathies, but he actually refrained from political comments and action during that trip.

On returning to London, he resumed his concert tour. On October 11, 1958, he became the first layperson, and the first black person, to take the pulpit in London's historic St. Paul's Cathedral, with a crowd of four thousand in attendance. He spoke briefly and sang spirituals, including "Jacob's Ladder" (now, like many Robeson clips, easily available on You Tube). The St. Paul appearance was one of the highlights of his resurgent glory. His reprisal of *Othello* the following year in Stratford, noted in Chapter Four, was another of those highlights.

Paul Robeson as Othello, 9 Apr 1898 - 23 Jan 1976, by Betsy Graves Reyneau, Oil on canvas, 1944.

During his *Othello* run, Robeson began making political speeches again. He spoke and sang at rallies for disarmament in London, and made a brief trip to Czechoslovakia to attend the Congress of Socialist Culture—an affirmation of his basic political ideology. He attended the World Youth Festival in Vienna, another predominantly communist led and organized event, but his remarks concerned the black struggles in America and South Africa. He made other brief trips throughout the European continent, including the communist nations of

Eastern Europe. But the seven-month run of *Othello,* Eslanda's worsening health problems and the overall stress of the years had begun to take a toll on an aging Paul Robeson.

In October 1960, the Robesons left on a long and grueling trip to Australia and New Zealand, earning more than $100,000, a welcome financial reward after almost a decade of economic stress resulting from the blacklist persecution in America. It would be his last extensive concert tour. In Australia, Robeson responded aggressively to hostile anti-communist questions from reporters, revealing the fervor of his leftist political views and the stress of the recent events on his emotional being. In New Zealand, he spoke out against American support of right-wing dictators like Chiang Kai-shek and Francisco Franco. He also discussed New Zealand's suppression of the indigenous Maori culture and in Australia he pointedly noted its government's egregious mistreatment of the Aborigine populations— a further expression of his commitment to the most marginalized groups in the world. His indignation, angrily expressed, was powerful and authentic.

After he returned to London, his emotional state took a turn for the worse. Although he continued to meet with old friends and political colleagues, to travel in the United Kingdom and the Continent, and to follow the developing events in the United States and throughout the world, he sank further into depression. He had begun to think seriously about his reutrn home to America. Instead, he decided to make another trip to the Soviet Union in March 1961. His first days there went well, at least on the surface. He met with old friends, greeted people on the streets, visited factories and gave interviews with the Soviet media. He appeared pleased to be back in friendly territory. He chatted with his wife by telephone from London about various plans and friends.

But the beginning of the end came shortly thereafter.

On March 27, 1961, after a party in Robeson's Moscow hotel room, he retreated into an inner room, and slashed his wrists with a razor blade. As Martin Duberman reports, Robeson's translator Irina found him on the floor and he was transported to the hospital. It remains unclear even now how close he was to death and the incident remains shrouded in mystery. Soviet doctors headed by psychiatrist Dr. Andrei Snezhnevsky treated him after this suicide attempt and after a month, he appeared somewhat improved. By early June, he was well enough to return to London, where his emotional state appeared to improve. But the interlude was brief and Eslanda arranged another trip to Moscow for additional medical and psychiatric treatment. After a three-month stay at the Barveekha Sanatorium in Moscow, he returned yet again to London, and again, his improvement was fleeting. Robeson soon entered his most serious and protracted psychiatric relapse.

AFTER BRIEFLY RETURNING TO LONDON PAUL WENT

BACK TO MOSCOW WHERE HE STAYED FOR THREE MONTHS AT A MENTAL HEALTH FACILITY. BACK IN LONDON, HE HAD A MAJOR PSYCHIATRIC RELAPSE!

AFTER BEING FOUND IN A FETAL POSITION, HE WAS ADMITTED TO THE PRIORY, A PRIVATE PSYCHIATRIC HOSPITAL. WHILE THERE, HE RECEIVED MORE THAN 50 ELECTROCONVULSIVE THERAPY TREATMENTS.

PAUL'S WIFE ESLANDA THOUGHT THAT HE WOULD RECEIVE BETTER TREATMENT AT THE BUCH CLINIC IN THE GERMAN DEMOCRATIC REPUBLIC (EAST GERMANY). DOCTORS FOUND HIM DEPRESSED AND LETHARGIC AND WITH SEVERAL PHYSICAL PROBLEMS.

PAUL ROBESON

RETURNED HOME TO THE UNITED STATES ON DECEMBER 22, 1963. WITH ALL OF HIS PHYSICAL AND EMOTIONAL PROBLEMS, PAUL STILL MANAGED TO ACCOMPLISH MUCH IN HIS LATER YEARS, EVEN SHOWING GREAT INTEREST IN THE EMERGING CIVIL RIGHTS MOVEMENT OF THE 1960's

Worrying about her husband's deteriorating emotional state, Eslanda had called their New York friend Helen Rosen in a panic. She flew immediately to London and the next morning found Paul in his bed, huddled in a fetal position, cowering and frightened. Eslanda made arrangements to have him admitted to the Priory, a private psychiatric facility with a stellar reputation. One of his doctors diagnosed him as a "manic depressive personality" and the medical staff decided on a course of electroconvulsive therapy (ECT). During his stay at Priory, Robeson received more than fifty administrations of ECT, which, while perhaps excessive under the circumstances, were still a standard treatment for depression in 1961. Robeson also received drug treatments but the range of medications was limited—far less than the range of psychiatric medications available in the early twenty-first century. At the Priory, he never received psychoanalytic or any other from of psychotherapy as part of his comprehensive treatment.

The electroconvulsive therapy sessions had some positive if temporary therapeutic effect. Robeson was permitted to make day visits to his London flat, but his deeper depression continued. By April 1961, he could make outings to the theater, while still shuttling back and forth for psychiatric treatment. The downward trajectory was becoming obvious.

After the long course of electroconvulsive treatments at the Priory, Eslanda, in consultation with family friends, decided that a better facility would be the Buch Clinic in East Berlin in the German Democratic Republic (East Germany). Doctors there found him depressed and without much personal drive or initiative. They also found various physical conditions not unusual for a sixty-five-year-old man. Although he made intermittent but temporary progress, his overall state remained problematic. Finally, in December 1963, he decided to return home to America for the final time, and on December 22, the Robesons boarded a flight from London to New York.

Paul Robeson, Jr. has long alleged that the US Central Intelligence Agency may have drugged his father during a visit to Moscow as well as influenced his ineffective treatment in the London hospital. Given a few late twentieth century revelations about the CIA, this view is not wholly implausible, but definitive evidence is unlikely to be discovered. The more likely scenario is that Robeson's mental illness resulted from several factors, including some organic causes involving bipolar depression, the onset of physical ailments, his wife's cancer diagnosis and deteriorating condition and the overwhelming strain of years of persecution and government harassment. All of this remains indeterminate, and remarkably, Paul Robeson accomplished so much despite his condition, even maintaining a strong interest in the growing civil rights movement.

Back home in Harlem, Robeson lived quietly.

His minimal energy rendered him unable to resume public life, including responding to hostile accounts of his return from the conservative media. In August 1964, he appeared and spoke briefly at the funeral of his close and longtime friend Ben Davis, the former communist councilman in New York City and Smith Act defendant. He made a few other public appearances, including the funeral of Lorraine Hansberry, the young playwright who died at thirty-four.

His major public appearance came at his sixty-seventh birthday celebration in New York. The "Salute" was a star-studded event, with an audience of two thousand, and celebrities including Ossie Davis, Pete Seeger, Dizzy Gillespie, James Baldwin and John Lewis, chairman of the Student Nonviolent Coordinating Committee (SNCC). Lewis, a major contemporary civil rights leader acknowledged Robeson's colossal contributions to civil liberties, and spoke of SNCC as, "Paul Robeson's spiritual children." Robeson then spoke for twenty-five minutes, using familiar language about the American and international freedom struggles. The response was overwhelmingly positive.

A subsequent trip to California marked the final turning point in Robeson's depressive state. He had a busy schedule in Los Angeles. He met with left-wing friends and associates, spoke briefly, and even sang a few songs. In San Francisco, his mental state deteriorated and Eslanda, struggling with terminal cancer, was exhausted. They returned to New York, where once again, he became lethargic and reserved. In June 1965, she found him holding scissors to his chest, with a superficial wound. He was admitted to Gracie Square psychiatric hospital, received medication, and discharged three weeks later. That September, he suffered from pneumonia and kidney blockage, compounding his fragile mental state. He was near death, but managed to survive. Eslanda's condition worsened, and on December 13, 1965, she died, two days before her seventieth birthday. Paul Robeson did not—or could not—attend her funeral.

THE 75TH BIRTHDAY CELEBRATION FOR PAUL ROBESON, ON APRIL 15, 1973 AT CARNEGIE HALL INCLUDED INFLUENTIAL GUESTS...

SUCH AS

ODETTA

DIZZY GILLESPIE

PETE SEEGER

AND MANY MORE

PAUL ROBESON'S FINAL 10 YEARS WERE SPENT IN THE HOME OF HIS SISTER MARIA ROBESON FORSYTHE. HE LIVED QUIETLY DURING THAT TIME, SEEING A FEW VISITORS, MOSTLY LONGTIME CLOSE FRIENDS. HE DIED IN 1976 AT THE AGE OF 77

Robeson spent his final years, from 1966 to 1976, in the West Philadelphia home of his sister Marian Robeson Forsythe, who had retired as a schoolteacher. He lived quietly during that time, seeing a few visitors, mostly longtime close personal friends, with his son serving as the effective gatekeeper. Citing ill health, he declined many invitations to attend events typical of his more robust years.

On April 15, 1973, Paul, Jr. coordinated his father's seventy-fifth birthday celebration in Carnegie Hall. Produced by Harry Belafonte, the event drew celebrities from the entertainment and political arenas, including Pete Seeger, Dizzy Gillespie, Odetta, Ossie Davis, Ruby Dee, Zero Mostel, Ramsey Clark, Angela Davis, Delores Huerta and others. World political leaders, including from third world nations of Africa, Asia and Latin America sent celebratory greetings to this festive affair. The emotional highlight came at the end of the program with a recorded message from Paul Robeson:

Though I have not been active for several years, I want you to know that I am the same Paul, dedicated as ever to the worldwide cause of humanity for freedom, peace and brotherhood. . . . I salute the colonial liberation movements of Africa, Latin America, and Asia, which have gained new inspiration and understanding from the heroic example of the Vietnamese people, who have once again turned back an imperialist aggressor. . . .

In Philadelphia, Robeson's health continued to decline. By the end of 1975, he had become seriously ill and finally, on January 23, 1976, he died from complications of a "severe cerebral vascular disorder." The funeral on January 27, 1976, was held in the Mother AME Zion Church in Harlem, where his brother Ben had served as pastor for twenty-seven years. Thousands gathered, including celebrities, old friends and political comrades, some political adversaries, and many complete strangers, especially ordinary African Americans from Harlem, who had quietly admired Paul Robeson for decades. A genuine champion of the people was laid to rest.

Paul Robeson left a majestic and lasting legacy to the world and to America. His stunning and largely unrivalled accomplishments as an athlete, artist and activist reflect

April, 9, 1898
Jan, 23, 1976

SINCE PAUL ROBESON'S DEATH IN 1976,

MANY EVENTS, CREATIVE DEVELOPMENTS, AND OTHER ACTIONS HAVE BROUGHT HIM BACK INTO PUBLIC RECOGNITION...

PAUL WAS AWARDED A GRAMMY, WHICH WAS ACCEPTED BY HIS SON

A PAUL ROBESON STAMP WAS ISSUED IN 2004

Grammy Lifetime Achievement Award

IN 1998 PAUL ROBESON CENTENNIAL CELEBRATIONS OCCURED THROUGH OUT THE WORLD!

AMONG OTHER ACKNOWLEDGEMENTS, PAUL HAS A STAR ON THE HOLLYWOOD WALK OF FAME.

THE BRILLIANT LEGACY OF PAUL ROBESON WILL ENDURE

PAUL ROBESON

those most American ideals and virtues: hard work, struggle, and above all, persistence in the face of adversity. For all the absurd allegations of his lack of loyalty and flawed citizenship, Paul Robeson's life was a patriotic American life in the finest sense of the phrase.

His athletic record has much to teach young athletes of the twenty-first century, especially those in major sports in highly visible university settings. Despite his athletic glories, Robeson always placed his academic achievements first, never forgetting the fundamental reason why he attended university in the first place.

As sociologist Harry Edwards has sharply noted, he refused to be a black gladiator in the service of a white capitalist elite.

As a stage actor, Robeson blazed the paths for generations of performers of color to grace the stage with roles more compatible with visions of human dignity. Likewise, in the legal profession and in the film industry, he understood and implemented the ideal of the "great refusal"—to abandon an enterprise rather than capitulate to its racism or to its denigration of decent standards of conduct. As a singer, Robeson exemplified the ideal of a socially conscious artist. Throughout his long career, he combined his performances with a powerful and humane social orientation, providing his audiences of millions with a progressive vision of politics, ethics and society. He inspired generations of other artists to do the same, an influence that can continue well into the present century.

But the realm of politics and morality is where Robeson's most profound legacy resides. His commitment to civil rights has yielded substantial progress, even though much more remains to be done. His lifelong struggle against racism in every form is a constant reminder of the need to continue in his path. Above all, Robeson's deep and abiding commitment to the welfare of all oppressed people has a powerful resonance in the early decades of the new century, with myriad human rights abuses still plaguing the world—dictatorial and brutal regimes, abuses and trafficking of women, persecutions of political prisoners, harassment and torture of gays and lesbians, grotesque exploitations of child labor, inadequate wages and horrific conditions for millions of working men and women, unacceptable hunger and poverty, outrageous rates of incarceration (including in the United States) and many more.

In his final recorded message at his seventy-fifth birthday celebration, Robeson quoted from his rewritten lyrics of "Ol' Man River":

> But I keeps laughin'
> Instead of cryin'
> I must keep fightin'
> Until I'm dyin'

Throughout his life, he fought tirelessly for the ideals that he expressed in those memorable lyrics. When he died, he passed his torch to a new generation of artists and activists who would continue the struggles for racial justice and human dignity. Those struggles are now the responsibility of socially engaged people facing the awesome challenges of the twenty-first century.

BIBLIOGRAPHY

Armentrout, Barbara, and Sterling Stuckey. 1999. *Paul Robeson's Living Legacy*. Chicago: Columbia College and Paul Robeson 100th Birthday Committee,.

Balaji, Murali. 2007. *The Professor and The Pupil: The Politics and Friendship of W.E.B. Du Bois and Paul Robeson*. New York: Nation Books.

Belafonte, Harry. 2011. *My Song*, New York: Alfred Knopf.

Bogle, Donald. 1995. *Toms, Coons, Mulattoes, Mammies, and Bucks: An Interpretive History of Blacks in American Film*. New York: Continuum Publishers,.

Boyle, Sheila Tully, and Andrew Bunie. 2001. *Paul Robeson: The Years of Promise and Achievement*. Amherst, MA: University of Massachusetts Press.

Brown, Lloyd. 1997. *The Young Paul Robeson*. Boulder, CO: Westview Press.

Caute, David. 1978. *The Great Fear: The Anti-Communist Purge Under Truman and Eisenhower*. New York: Simon and Schuster.

Davis, Lenwood. 1982. *A Paul Robeson Research Guide*. Westport, CT: Greenwood Press.

Dorinson, Joseph and William Pencak, eds. 2002. *Paul Robeson: Essays on His Life and Legacy*. Jefferson, NC: McFarland Company.

Duberman, Martin. 1988. *Paul Robeson*. New York: Alfred Knopf.

Editors of Freedomways. 1998. *Paul Robeson: The Great Forerunner*. New York: International Publishers.

Foner, Henry, ed. 1978. *Paul Robeson Speaks*. New York: Citadel Press.

Hill, Errol. 1981. *Shakespeare in Sable*. Amherst, MA: University of Massachusetts Press.

Holmes, Burnam. 1995. *Paul Robeson: A Voice of Struggle*. Austin, TX: Raintree Steck-Vaughn.

Paul Robeson Foundation. 1998. *Paul Robeson: Bearer of a Culture* (exhibition catalogue). New York: The Paul Robeson Foundation with the New York Historical Society.

Ransby, Barbara. 2013. *Eslanda: The Large and Unconventional Life of Mrs. Paul Robeson*. New Haven: Yale University Press.

Robeson, Paul. 1988. *Here I Stand*. Boston: Beacon Press.

Robeson, Paul, Jr. 2001. *The Undiscovered Paul Robeson: An Artist's Journey, 1898-1939*. New York: John Wiley and Sons.

Robeson, Paul, Jr. 2010. *The Undiscovered Paul Robeson: Quest for Freedom, 1939-1976*. New York: John Wiley and Sons.

Robeson, Susan. 1981. *The Whole World in His Hands*. Secaucus, NJ: Citadel Press.

Swindall, Lindsey. 2013. *Paul Robeson: A Life of Activism and Art*. Lanham, MD: Rowman and Littlefield.

Swindall, Lindsey. 2011. *The Politics of Paul Robeson's Othello*. Jackson, MS: University of Mississippi Press.

Stewart, Jeffrey, ed. 1998. *Paul Robeson: Artist and Citizen*. New Brunswick, NJ: Rutgers University Press.

Stuckey, Sterling. 1984 (reprint). *"I Want to be African": Paul Robeson and The Ends of Nationalist Practice and Theory, 1919-1945*. Los Angeles: UCLA Center for Afro American Studies.

SELECTED CHRONOLOGY

1898 Paul Robeson is born in Princeton, New Jersey, April 9, 1898.

1904 His mother, Maria Louisa Bustill Robeson, dies in an accidental fire.

1915 Robeson graduates from Somerville High School and wins a four-year scholarship to Rutgers College.

He tries out for the varsity football team at Rutgers and is injured by players who do not want an African American player on the squad; he returns and makes the team, later becoming a two-time All-American star.

1918 Robeson is elected to Phi Beta Kappa at Rutgers.

His father, Rev. William Drew Robeson, dies.

1919 Robeson graduates from Rutgers, having won 15 varsity letters (football, baseball, basketball, and track) and delivers a commencement address, as class valedictorian, on "The New Idealism."

He enters New York University Law School and transfers mid academic year to Columbia University Law School.

1920 Robeson makes stage debut in *Simon the Cyrenian* at the Harlem YMCA.

He begins his professional football career on week-ends with the Akron Pros, ending two years later with the Milwaukee Badgers.

1921 Robeson marries Eslanda Cardoza Goode.

1922 Robeson performs in the plays *Taboo* and *Shuffle Along*.

1923 Robeson graduates from Columbia Law School and works briefly in the firm of Louis W. Stotesbury, resigning after a white secretary refuses to take dictation from him.

1924 Robeson stars on stage in Eugene O'Neill's *The Emperor Jones* and *All God's Chillun Got Wings*.

He begins his film career in Oscar Micheaux's *Body and Soul*.

1925 Robeson gives his first singing concert with Lawrence Brown as his accompanist.

1927 Paul Robeson, Jr. is born.

1928 Robeson plays in *Show Boat* and sings Ol' Man River in London.

1930 Robeson performs in Shakespeare's *Othello* for the first time in London.

1933 Robeson stars in the film version of *Emperor Jones*.

1934 Robeson stars in *Sanders of the River.*

He makes his first visit to the Soviet Union and is extremely impressed by his friendly reception and by what he observes.

1935 Robeson appears in the play *Stevedore* and the film *Show Boat.*

1937 Robeson emerges as a political activist by supporting the Spanish Republic against the fascist rebellion by General Francisco Franco. He declares, "The artist must take sides. He must elect to fight for freedom or for slavery."

He co-founds, with Max Yergan, the Council on African Affairs (CAA), which becomes the leading organization opposing colonialism in Africa.

1938 Robeson goes to Spain and sings to soldiers fighting for the Spanish Republic in the Spanish Civil War.

1939 Robeson sings "Ballad fir Americans" for CBS radio and later at the Hollywood Bowl in Los Angeles.

He stars in *Proud Valley*, his favorite film role.

1941 Federal Bureau of Investigation, under Director J. Edgar Hoover, begins gathering information about Robeson's activities.

1943 Robeson stars in the Broadway production of *Othello*, which has a run of 296 performances.

He leads a delegation to the Commissioner of Baseball asking for the inclusion of black players in the major leagues.

1945 Robeson receives the Springarn Medal from the NAACP.

1946 Robeson leads a delegation to see President Harry Truman to support anti-lynching legislation. The President tells the group that the time is not ripe for such action.

He appears before a California legislative committee on Un-American Activities and denies that he is a Communist and criticizes the discriminatory treatment of African Americans.

1948 Robeson campaigns for Henry Wallace, the presidential candidate of the Progressive Party in the 1948 election.

1949 Robeson ends a concert in Moscow by singing a song of the Warsaw Ghetto resistance, "Zog Nit Keynmol," in Yiddish. He receives thunderous applause from the Soviet audience.

He attends the World Partisans of Peace Congress in Paris, where his statements on peace with the Soviet Union are misrepresented in the U.S. media.

An anti-Semitic, anti-black mob disrupts a Robeson concert in Peekskill, New York. One week later. Robeson sings in Peekskill with a large security force of union members. Another angry mob attacks concert visitors while police officials stand by and do nothing to prevent the violence.

1950 The U.S. State Department takes away Robeson's passport, keeping him in internal exile for the next eight years.

1952 Roberson gives a concert to 40,000 at the Peace Arch at the Canadian border after officials stop him from entering Canada.

He receives the Stalin Peace Prize from the Soviet Union.

1956 Robeson appears before the House Un-American Activities Committee and responds defiantly to questions about his associations and his political affiliations.

1958 Robeson publishes *Here I Stand,* a book that combines autobiographical and political material.

The U.S. Supreme Court rules that the State Department lacks the right to revoke citizens' passports because of their political beliefs. This decision allows Robeson to regain his passport and his right to travel.

He gives concerts in England, Wales, the Soviet Union, and East Germany.

1959 Robeson performs *Othello* in Stratford-upon-Avon, England for the third and final time.

1960 Robeson travels to Australia and New Zealand for his final concert tour and also makes political comments in both nations.

1961 Robeson is hospitalized in Moscow following a suicide attempt.

1963 Robeson returns to the United States after extended psychiatric treatments in England and East Germany.

1965 Eslanda Robeson dies at the age of 69.

1966 Robeson moves to Philadelphia to live with his sister, Marian Robeson Forsyth, for his final years.

1973 The 75th birthday celebration of Paul Robeson is held in New York at Carnegie Hall, with many celebrities and with a taped message from Robeson, saying "I am the same Paul, dedicated as ever to the worldwide cause of humanity for freedom, peace, and brotherhood."

1976 Robeson dies on January 23 in Philadelphia. His funeral is at the Mother A.M.E. Zion Church in Harlem on January 27.

about the author and illustrators

PAUL VON BLUM is Senior Lecturer in African American Studies and Communication Studies at UCLA. He has taught at the University of California since 1968, serving 11 years at UC Berkeley before arriving at UCLA in 1980. He is the author of six books and numerous articles on art, culture, education, and politics. His most recent book is *A Life at the Margins: Keeping the Political Vision*; his 2011 memoir that chronicles almost 50 years of political activism, starting with his civil rights work in the South and elsewhere in the early 1960s.

ELIZABETH VON NOTIAS was trained professionally at the California Institute of the Arts and at the Art Institute of California in Los Angeles, with a focus on graphic design. She has shown her work in several individual and group exhibitions throughout the Southern California region and her works are in many private collections.

RAMSESS is a self taught artist who works in multiple media ranging from ink to acrylic to mosaic to glass to cloth. As an ardent fan and lover of blues and jazz music, much of his art is a reflection of that love, honoring the musicians and the music they create. Throughout the year, Ramsess can be found at many of the national jazz and blues festivals.

THE FOR BEGINNERS® SERIES

AFRICAN HISTORY FOR BEGINNERS:	ISBN 978-1-934389-18-8
ANARCHISM FOR BEGINNERS:	ISBN 978-1-934389-32-4
ARABS & ISRAEL FOR BEGINNERS:	ISBN 978-1-934389-16-4
ART THEORY FOR BEGINNERS:	ISBN 978-1-934389-47-8
ASTRONOMY FOR BEGINNERS:	ISBN 978-1-934389-25-6
AYN RAND FOR BEGINNERS:	ISBN 978-1-934389-37-9
BARACK OBAMA FOR BEGINNERS, AN ESSENTIAL GUIDE:	ISBN 978-1-934389-44-7
BEN FRANKLIN FOR BEGINNERS:	ISBN 978-1-934389-48-5
BLACK HISTORY FOR BEGINNERS:	ISBN 978-1-934389-19-5
THE BLACK HOLOCAUST FOR BEGINNERS:	ISBN 978-1-934389-03-4
BLACK WOMEN FOR BEGINNERS:	ISBN 978-1-934389-20-1
CHOMSKY FOR BEGINNERS:	ISBN 978-1-934389-17-1
DADA & SURREALISM FOR BEGINNERS:	ISBN 978-1-934389-00-3
DANTE FOR BEGINNERS:	ISBN 978-1-934389-67-6
DECONSTRUCTION FOR BEGINNERS:	ISBN 978-1-934389-26-3
DEMOCRACY FOR BEGINNERS:	ISBN 978-1-934389-36-2
DERRIDA FOR BEGINNERS:	ISBN 978-1-934389-11-9
EASTERN PHILOSOPHY FOR BEGINNERS:	ISBN 978-1-934389-07-2
EXISTENTIALISM FOR BEGINNERS:	ISBN 978-1-934389-21-8
FDR AND THE NEW DEAL FOR BEGINNERS:	ISBN 978-1-934389-50-8
FOUCAULT FOR BEGINNERS:	ISBN 978-1-934389-12-6
GENDER & SEXUALITY FOR BEGINNERS:	ISBN 978-1-934389-69-0
GLOBAL WARMING FOR BEGINNERS:	ISBN 978-1-934389-27-0
GREEK MYTHOLOGY FOR BEGINNERS:	ISBN 978-1-934389-83-6
HEIDEGGER FOR BEGINNERS:	ISBN 978-1-934389-13-3
THE HISTORY OF OPERA FOR BEGINNERS:	ISBN 978-1-934389-79-9
ISLAM FOR BEGINNERS:	ISBN 978-1-934389-01-0
JANE AUSTEN FOR BEGINNERS:	ISBN 978-1-934389-61-4
JUNG FOR BEGINNERS:	ISBN 978-1-934389-76-8
KIERKEGAARD FOR BEGINNERS:	ISBN 978-1-934389-14-0
LACAN FOR BEGINNERS:	ISBN 978-1-934389-39-3
LINGUISTICS FOR BEGINNERS:	ISBN 978-1-934389-28-7
MALCOLM X FOR BEGINNERS:	ISBN 978-1-934389-04-1
MARX'S *DAS KAPITAL* FOR BEGINNERS:	ISBN 978-1-934389-59-1
MCLUHAN FOR BEGINNERS:	ISBN 978-1-934389-75-1
NIETZSCHE FOR BEGINNERS:	ISBN 978-1-934389-05-8
PHILOSOPHY FOR BEGINNERS:	ISBN 978-1-934389-02-7
PLATO FOR BEGINNERS:	ISBN 978-1-934389-08-9
POETRY FOR BEGINNERS:	ISBN 978-1-934389-46-1
POSTMODERNISM FOR BEGINNERS:	ISBN 978-1-934389-09-6
RELATIVITY & QUANTUM PHYSICS FOR BEGINNERS:	ISBN 978-1-934389-42-3
SARTRE FOR BEGINNERS:	ISBN 978-1-934389-15-7
SHAKESPEARE FOR BEGINNERS:	ISBN 978-1-934389-29-4
STRUCTURALISM & POSTSTRUCTURALISM FOR BEGINNERS:	ISBN 978-1-934389-10-2
WOMEN'S HISTORY FOR BEGINNERS:	ISBN 978-1-934389-60-7
UNIONS FOR BEGINNERS:	ISBN 978-1-934389-77-5
U.S. CONSTITUTION FOR BEGINNERS:	ISBN 978-1-934389-62-1
ZEN FOR BEGINNERS:	ISBN 978-1-934389-06-5
ZINN FOR BEGINNERS:	ISBN 978-1-934389-40-9

www.forbeginnersbooks.com